Diversity Includes Disability

Diversity Includes Disability
Perspectives on the U-M Council
for Disability Concerns

**Anna Ercoli Schnitzer
and Bonnie A. Dede**

University of Michigan, Ann Arbor, MI, USA

Published in the United States of America by
Michigan Publishing

DOI: http://dx.doi.org/10.3998/mpub.9997270

ISBN 978-1-60785-478-4 (paper)
ISBN 978-1-60785-479-1 (e-book)

An imprint of Michigan Publishing, Maize Books serves the publishing
needs of the University of Michigan community by making high-quality
scholarship widely available in print and online. It represents a new model
for authors seeking to share their work within and beyond the academy,
offering streamlined selection, production, and distribution processes.
Maize Books is intended as a complement to more formal modes of
publication in a wide range of disciplinary areas.

http://www.maizebooks.org

On the cover:

Left: The kick-off event of our October 2005 Investing in Ability program: A line-up on the U-M Diag of service-dogs-to-be and their fostering parents.

Right: Two members of the Detroit DieHard Wheelchair Basketball team with a young spectator participating at the U-M Army-Navy Wheelchair Basketball Game, October 2016.

Contents

Background

In view of the fact that no official narrative has been written about the U-M Council for Disability Concerns (CFDC) in its thirty five-year history as a campus advocacy organization for accessibility and disability issues, the Bicentennial Year of the University of Michigan seemed an ideal time to write one to add to the institutional history.

Disability, a universal human condition, appears in its varied aspects in every place of the world. A particularly problematic situation often occurs in academe where disabled individuals, because of the pace, competition, and finances involved with obtaining a degree or achieving advancement in their positions, may have considerable difficulty in achieving their desired goals.

A recent special report of *The Chronicle of Higher Education*, "Diversity in Academe: Disability on Campus," September 18, 2016,

> examines the challenges that students, academics, and colleges face in dealing with disability on campus. It includes the voices of people who struggle with physical disabilities that make it difficult to navigate older buildings and lovely grounds, and of others who have less-visible conditions such as bipolar or autism-spectrum disorders. Some scholars, having learned how to manage their own conditions, have built successful academic careers despite having blanked out in the middle of a speech or being forced to suddenly cancel class or take a medical leave. Our coverage also reflects some continuing debates relating to disability, including whether the philosophy of universal design—design that is meant to benefit everybody—sufficiently accommodates those with special needs.

To address these concerns, the CFDC was established at the University of Michigan to overcome, or at least mitigate, obstacles while providing advocacy and support to individuals with disabilities, to increase accessibility to all campus services, and thus ultimately to educate the campus about and destigmatize disability.

> "For too long, disability has been constructed as the antithesis of higher education, often positioned as a distraction, a drain, a problem to be solved. The ethic of higher education encourages students and teachers alike to accentuate ability, valorize perfection, and stigmatize anything that hints at intellectual, mental, or physical weakness, even as we gesture toward the value of diversity and innovation." Timothy Dolmage in "Academic Ableism: Disability and Higher Education," argues that disability is actually central to higher education and that

building more inclusive schools allows better education for all. Further, in "Negotiating Disability: Disclosure and Higher Education," the editors state: "Disability is not always central to claims about diversity and inclusion in higher education but should be . . . While disclosing one's disability and identifying shared experience can engender moments of solidarity, the situation is always complicated by the intersecting factors of race and ethnicity, gender, sexuality, and class."

The University of Michigan's CFDC has been in existence for over thirty years. Although technically outside the traditional definition of a departmental team unit, this organization epitomizes a collaborative, multi-person, multidisciplinary, multipurpose cohesive effort focused on the important topics of accessibility and disability. Its services have been recognized and appreciated over the years by numerous individuals in the campus community, including members of the U-M Board of Regents, as well as in the surrounding local area.

Establishment of the U-M Council for Disability

Established in 1983 by then University President Harold Shapiro at the conclusion of the University of Michigan's observance of the 1982 International Year of Disabled Persons (IYDP), the CFDC was created to act in an advisory capacity to the Director of Affirmative Action regarding university programs and policies affecting people with disabilities. The primary responsibilities of the new council were to improve accessibility on the campus, to develop scholarships for students with disabilities, and to provide linkage between people and units involved with disability issues. To address this mandate, the council initially created two task forces: **Accessibility** and **Education**. Then, in 1988, a third unit, the **Employment Task Force**, was established. Originally, the council had only about a dozen members; then the membership rapidly grew to include forty-four (two students, five faculty, thirty-seven staff). Today, the council has almost 300 members on its mailing list, over 200 of whom are U-M affiliates and the others who are interested members of the local community.

Early Mission Statement and Subsequent Action Plan of the U-M CFDC

As the council approaches its fifth decade, its members look to its original Mission Statement as a guide:

- **Promote** the development of a physical and social environment that provides full access of programs, services, and facilities to every person in the university community (students, faculty, staff, guests).

- **Advance** the university's commitment to the quality of experience for all persons, including those with disabilities.
- **Act** in an advisory capacity to recommend university programs and policies that assure full opportunity and access to qualified individuals with disabilities.
- **Advocate** for the concerns of members of the university community who have disabilities.
- **Educate** the university community by increasing our awareness of and sensitivity to all issues related to individuals who have disabilities.

Development of the council's **Strategic Plan** was initiated in January 2003 and was informed by two goals. First, surveying the council stakeholders as to the issues and challenges facing people with disabilities in the University of Michigan community would clarify the most pressing problems facing people with disabilities. Second, developing a systematic approach to overcoming these challenges would focus council efforts, giving the council the chance to have the greatest impact using the resources at its disposal. Identifying specific actions would lead in a stepwise fashion to overcoming identified problems.

A group of graduate students undertook to survey the council members and other stakeholders in the disability community, including staff and students. In addition to identifying broader areas of concern and the perceived role of the council, survey respondents gave a wealth of information that led to the generation of a council-updated vision statement. The council members then articulated the core problems facing people with disabilities, as well as some of the causes of those core problems, to clarify the barriers holding the university back from promoting accessibility. **Two core problems in the university community and leadership emerged:**

1. General lack of awareness in the university community and leadership of disability issues—stemming in part from limited council visibility and resources—and

2. Inconsistent enforcement of ambiguous policies promoting accommodations and accessibility.

It was also recognized that these core problems were exacerbated by diminished attention to the accessibility needs of the university faculty and staff and that these challenges precluded and produced a climate that was not consistently welcoming of—and often inhospitable to—people with disabilities. These core problems then served to prioritize for the council many issues that surfaced from stakeholder survey responses. Subsequently, **two broad council objectives developed in the winter of 2003, which were to**

1. Increase awareness and education through
   - Increasing general awareness among the general university community,
   - Increasing specific knowledge among university leadership,
   - Substantiating disability issues, and
   - Mobilizing resources to support the council's work and
2. Promote consistent university disability policy interpretation.

The core problems identified in the survey together with prioritized council objectives were then matched with potential action steps that the council could undertake over the next few years, given current resource constraints. Finally, several council members met to refine and clarify core problems, council objectives, and possible actions. These were further reviewed and explored by a variety of campus experts to ensure action steps were aligned with and complemented other disability advocacy activities occurring in the university:

Core Problem 1: Limited Education and Awareness of Disability Issues Exist in the Community. Concerns Persist by Service Providers and Service Consumers. CFDC Effectiveness Is Hampered by Limited Visibility

Council Objective 1A: Increasing General Awareness about Disability and Accessibility through Education of Various Campus Populations

CFDC Action Plan (Survey Core Problem 1, Council Objective 1A—Increase Awareness and Education):

- Make the council better known as a resource, where council members serve as ambassadors, acting as a source of information and a gateway for advice and feedback on disability issues.
- Get disability on people's agendas. Enhance awareness and education on campus and in the community throughout the year about disability issues and concerns.

Action areas:

- Create brochure for all employees of the university, faculty, and staff, as well as all students—for entire university community.

- Provide and disseminate syllabus language for use by faculty.
- Promote the idea that every letter of admission includes language about disability and accommodations.
- Partner with groups that are responsible for promoting full accessibility to disseminate information/resources, policies, and ideas about low-cost solutions for accommodations for all staff and students at all levels—for example, use *The Michigan Daily* and the website for dissemination of ideas. These groups could include Human Resources, Occupational Health Services, Michigan Medicine, MWorks, occupational therapists, and Services for Students with Disabilities (SSD).
- Partner with the University of Michigan Initiative in Disability Studies (UMInDS) in establishing and promoting a Disability Studies Program at the university.
- Partner with groups and programs currently promoting diversity, inclusion, and multiculturalism, such as Spectrum Center (LGBT), IGR, CRLT, diversity dialogues, and work-based diversity committees, to assist them in achieving and maintaining competence in the area of disability awareness.
- (Year 1) Identify training needs of council members interested in promoting targeted education and awareness; generate resources to support such capacity building among the council members; and identify target audiences for proactive education efforts.
- (Year 2) Implement targeted education efforts.

Council Objective 1B: Increasing Specific
Information about Disability among Leadership

a. University leadership

Educating university leaders and increasing council access to leaders through intentional linkages:

CFDC Action Plan (Survey Core Problem 1, Council Objective 1B—University Leadership):

- To advocate and promote access for full and equal participation for all persons in all university activities, the council will educate and advise university leaders, through closer linkage with top administrators, keeping administration informed about council concerns and disability issues.

Action areas:

- Prioritize university leadership that the council will approach; articulate limited numbers (top three) of key council concerns and disability issues to be presented.
- Communicate with/write position paper to the president, deans, and so on.
- Meet with the president
- Meet annually with the deans
- Institute regular reporting relationship with the University Diversity Council or Assistant Provost Assistant Deans' Group (APADG) and Academic Services Board (ASB), and all vice presidents (VPs).
- Promote the creation of Office of Vice Provost for Disability Concerns, with the council becoming an advisory body to this office.

b.   University facilities leadership

Increasing accessibility of university facilities:

CFDC Action Plan (Survey Core Problem 1, Council Objective 1B—University Facilities Leadership):

- Encourage change to building structures on campus so they will be truly accessible and not merely "up to code."
- Become proactive in establishing links, for example, with the U-M facilities operation and achieve more collaboration with managers of facilities and other departments—those individuals who have the authority to make changes.
- Promote universal accessibility of all university websites and adaptive computing technology.

Action areas:

- Advocate for a full-time, permanent position to serve as a liaison with campus construction projects to ensure that new and renovated facilities are fully accessible and that all projects include plans for accessibility during the construction phase.
- Promote recognized standards of website accessibility on all official university websites.
- Provide feedback to and advise the Software Usability/Accessibility Specialist in work related to university website accessibility.

Council Objective 1C: Substantiating Issues
Related to Disability and Accessibility

CFDC Action Plan (Survey Core Problem 1, Council Objective 1C—Disability Issues):

- The council will give a voice to our constituents, helping define the needs among faculty, staff, and students; evaluating current services; and assessing current policies and their implementation and enforcement.

Action areas:

- Collect information/suggestions from faculty, staff, and student via forums, interviews, and visits to CFDC meetings.
- Officially request a Task Force, sponsored by the Vice President of Student Affairs or the Provost, to look into the satisfaction level of current students with disabilities and to create a comprehensive plan to address concerns.
- Research surveys and data—write reports that get endorsed as a mandate.

Council Objective 1D: Mobilizing Resources—
Generate Resources to Enable Council's Pursuit of Its
Mission and Accomplishment of Its Objectives

CFDC Action Plan (Survey Core Problem 1, Council Objective 1D—Resources):

- Identify areas of weakness and obtain and maintain resources (money) to remedy, work toward obtaining an annual budget, and push for centralized funding for needed accommodations for faculty and staff at all levels.
- Keep adaptive technology computing sites (ATCSs) up to date. Employ a full-time adaptive technologist at the university. The university should help secure loans for use of adaptive technology for students and staff.

Action areas:

- Identify peer institutions and survey them with specific questions concerning funding for accessibility. How do other institutions budget for accessibility?
- Find other mechanisms of funding CFDC—check with others who represent other constituents.

- Obtain an ongoing budget for the council, either through central funding or development.
- Bring in quality speakers.
- Obtain additional funding when necessary.

Core Problem 2: New Policies Addressing Nondiscrimination for Staff and Faculty Give University Administrators Much More Latitude than Past Policies to Decide What Constitutes Reasonable Accommodations

Council Objective 2: Increasing Consistency in Baseline Interpretation of University Policies Related to Nondiscrimination and Reasonable Accommodation of Faculty and Staff with Disabilities.

CFDC Action Plan (Survey Core Problem 2, Council Objective 2— Promote Consistent University Disability Policy Interpretation):

Action areas:

- Education and increased awareness.
- Define disability: "This is what we're talking about." Frame disability in terms commonly found in the "diversity" discourse.
- Review and reference previous policies and procedures used in departments as guides to interpreting new policies.
- Develop Executive Officer–level credibility (President, VPs, Regents).
- Advise Executive Office levels regarding policy development, interpretation, and consistent application.
- Liaison with each school, college, and area.
- Serve to problem-solve and share/disseminate information.

Early History of the CFDC

A confidential four-part survey had been conducted by council members in November 1990 to discover how well students with disabilities were able to participate in the classroom, in the university, as well as the community environment, and the strategies they have developed to overcome barriers. The sections included health status, the environment, level of participation, and personal background of each participant. According to the council archives, a U-M needs' assessment among students had been performed in 1974, and the number of students with disabilities in need of special services had increased by 87%, according to data from the Big Ten Universities, during the 1994–1999 period.

In its earlier years (1993–1998), the council conducted most of its work through three task forces: **Accessibility, Education,** and **Employment.** Some of the highlights of the accomplishments of the **Accessibility Task Force** during this period were improving the physical accessibility of facilities throughout the campus by removing architectural barriers. This process was improved to the point that problematic issues were addressed within a short period of time if they were easily fixed and tracked by the task force if longer range solutions were required, with the number of problems requiring tracking continuing to decrease as new buildings were constructed and major renovation projects completed. A campus accessibility map was created and updated to assist individuals in finding the best route to and from buildings, to identify accessible entrances and restrooms, to mark the location of elevators, and to indicate parking areas for those with valid handicap parking permits. The **Accessibility Task Force** continued to work on ways for graduation and other public ceremonies to be more accessible for everyone attending.

Early leaders of the council and its task forces included Edward Loyer, Brian Clapham, Lee Pastalan, Sandra Cole, Marilyn Dietrich, Yeheskel Hasenfeld, John Hagen, Patrick C. West, Jayne Thorson, and Patricia Whitfield. Membership consisted of representatives from multiple university units, these often being the directors and managers of the unit.

The **Education Task Force** was formed to address special situations encountered by students with disabilities in academic and related university programs. It emphasized equitable opportunities for disabled students to achieve success. Working with the Office of the Services for Students with Disabilities, the **Education Task Force** created an informative video and a Faculty Handbook to assist faculty members working with students with disabilities both in the classroom and the laboratory. It also produced and distributed a brochure titled "Students with Psychiatric Disabilities; An Informational Guide for Students, Staff, and Faculty at the University of Michigan," describing the university's legal obligations related to academic accommodations for these students and listing campus resources available to deal with specific situations. Over 5,000 copies of an equivalent guide, addressed to supervisors, were distributed in 1997 on the Ann Arbor, Flint, and Dearborn campuses. Another area addressed was that of internships and field placement programs for students with disabilities. The **Education Task Force,** in conjunction with the Office of the Provost and Executive Vice President for Academic Affairs, provided written information and individual consultation to academic units to assist them in meeting the legal and practical considerations regarding student internship opportunities.

With the increasing use of computer technology both in teaching and conducting research, it became essential for all students to have proper access to computers to succeed, so the **Education Task Force** members worked with the Undergraduate Library, the Office of Student Affairs, the Information Technology Division (ITD), and Herman Miller, Inc., to design a state-of-the-art site with equipment required by students with a variety of disabilities. As a result of this multi-partnership effort, an adaptive technology computing site (ATCS), now having evolved and later renamed the James Edward Knox Adaptive Technology Computing Site (Knox Center), opened in 1997 in the Shapiro Undergraduate Library. The ATCS featured nine ergonomically designed workstations with computer technology to accommodate various disabilities.

The goal of the **Employment Task Force**, as its name indicates, was to identify and remove barriers to equal employment. Much of this work involved training supervisors about the legal requirements of the Americans with Disabilities Act (ADA) and educating them about stereotypes that are prevalent about persons with disabilities. The first visible product of the group was a printed reference handbook *Americans with Disabilities Act (ADA) Resource Packet* and the second was a video "Focus on Abilities. The ADA at the University of Michigan," which was revised in 1998. Both resources were intended to illustrate how supervisors can accommodate employees with disabilities. In 1994, the members revised and expanded the Physician's Statement, a four-page form used to collect and document relevant information about an employee's health condition to determine whether any job accommodation is needed. The **Employment Task Force** was also interested in developing written materials and a web page on ergonomics by working with a team of experts to design cost-effective solutions to workplace ergonomic issues and to provide relevant resources in electronic format.

Personal Histories of Various Outstanding, Early Council Members

Over the years, various council members have contributed their expertise to the entire university disability community, providing human interest and unique documentation. One superb example of such an individual is **Joan E. Smith (Joni), the recipient of the first James T. Neubacher Award.** Now retired but never forgotten and still attending monthly council meetings, Joni has maintained a large, heavy packing box full of grateful and appreciative notes and letters of people for whom she has provided sign language interpretation over the years. She has a large collection of both casual clippings and formal congratulatory messages from all over campus and from nonaffiliates who are deaf or who have deaf family members. Joni has served as the interpreter for an astounding number of politicians and other public figures, including the Dalai Lama, who presented her with a white scarf after telling the audience these encouraging words: "Take care of heart and mind while acquiring knowledge."

Here is Joni in her own words followed by a typical letter of appreciation (see Photo 1) for all that she has done over many years for the hearing-impaired individuals in our campus community and their families.

Do you remember me? I am Joan E. Smith, a longtime employee of the University and the sign language interpreter for many, many years. Do you remember that Bill Gosling and I are good friends, both collecting pop-up books? My nephew is Robert Sabuda, "The Michelangelo of pop-up books," according to the New York Times. Yes, I remember interpreting for you, the first male administrator with a pierced ear and a twinkle in his eye. We hope you are well and have received all the recognition you so richly deserve. You always belonged at the top of the list, in my opinion.

In view of our University of Michigan Bicentennial this year, I believe that I have some relevant human experiences to add to the history. I hope that you will consider capturing this account in some way and offering it to the current members of our community as part of a diversity and inclusion initiative begun long, long ago.

I began working as a sign language interpreter at the University of Michigan in 1986 when the first deaf student, Jose Irizarry, was accepted into our student body. He met many, many Deaf individuals from all over the country while at U-M through a project with Kresge Hearing Research that took place at Gallaudet University. Incidentally, I still keep in touch with him and now he is married with several children. To give you a little information about the U-M's first deaf student: Jose went to Wisconsin Law School and later so did his wife, Jane Coffee. Jose was adopted by his stepfather and subsequently changed his last name. Our daughter Jennifer, and son Jeremy both went with us for the long weekend and we danced at their wedding in Kohler, Wisconsin. Their wedding was packed with Deaf Professionals who waved white handkerchiefs, whirling them instead of clapping. I have to report that they looked like Whirling Dervishes in the dim lights of the ceremony. It was breathtaking. They hired two interpreters, one of whom was Bambi Rhiel. Jose works for the Federal Government and Jane is a practicing attorney in Washington, D.C. They are both very active in the Deaf Professional community in D.C. and are members of the A.G. Bell National Organization. Jose and Jane play in the Deaf Baseball teams in D.C. Jose once brought his youngest son here for a tour of the U-M, staying with our daughter Jennifer. Needless to say, we were so happy to see them that we all celebrated as if they were close relatives.

Since those humble beginnings with the first deaf student, the U-M has worked to attract and include more and more deaf and hard of hearing individuals, about 25 students in the beginning and even more currently. In fact, as you know, we now have several deaf professors and are always keeping the door open for more. For example, Dr. Philip Zazove, Chair of the Department of Family Medicine in the Medical Center, is an amazing mentor to our deaf and hard of hearing students. His more than 20 years of service, attending deaf events, writing letters of reference, teaching medical students all about deafness, being an enthusiastic advocate, and following through with students—all spread the word and make him very popular and a kind of guru of deafness. His history as the "Deaf Doctor" at U-M's Shady Trails Camp in Northport, is often repeated and taken back to their own communities by deaf students who attended their first camp in the 1990s and marveled at discovering a doctor who understands and speaks their language. Deaf patients travel from all over Michigan to see him. A former member of the Board of Directors for Ann Arbor Center for Independent Living, Dr. Zazove continues his quest of making things more accessible for all people. He is always on the look out for prospective deaf and hard of hearing students and faculty members to attract to our University. He was awarded The James T. Neubacher Award by the Council for Disability Concerns in 1998 and at the time was one of only four Deaf physicians practicing in the United States.

www.uofmhealth.org/news/archive/201211/deaf-pioneer-now -department-chair-accomplished-physician

Another memory I have was of Carlos Lamus, who employed at U-M as a janitor at the time. I was told by some students that he was being forced to wear a nametag saying, "I am Deaf." Being outraged, I stormed over to the Michigan Union to remedy this injustice. He put up his hand, using the "Stop," sign and explained that he cleaned the women's restroom, and always put the appropriate sign in front of the door to indicate that the area was being cleaned. However, the female students ignored the sign and continued to come in anyway. When they encountered him, they would scream and carry on. For this reason, he requested the nametag and would point to it when necessary. Also, I interpreted for his marriage in a park and then years later also interpreted for his divorce. All the members of his family were all professionals except him.

Although I have been retired for several years now, I remember vividly having the "dream job" of signing at major university events for well-known people, for example, former President Bill Clinton and former First Lady Hillary Clinton among many other government officials and internationally-known personalities.

The Dalai Lama Makes an Appearance in Ann Arbor for the Wallenberg Lecture

On April 21, 1994, despite the busy exam week, many students and faculty mingled with a crowd of over 10,000 entering Crisler Arena for the fourth Wallenberg Lecture, delivered by the Dalai Lama. He spoke to his Ann Arbor audience of the goal for humanity in the twenty-first century, which is "to build a happier world." However, for this dream to be fulfilled,

Photo 1 A typical letter of appreciation for Joan E. Smith (Joni)

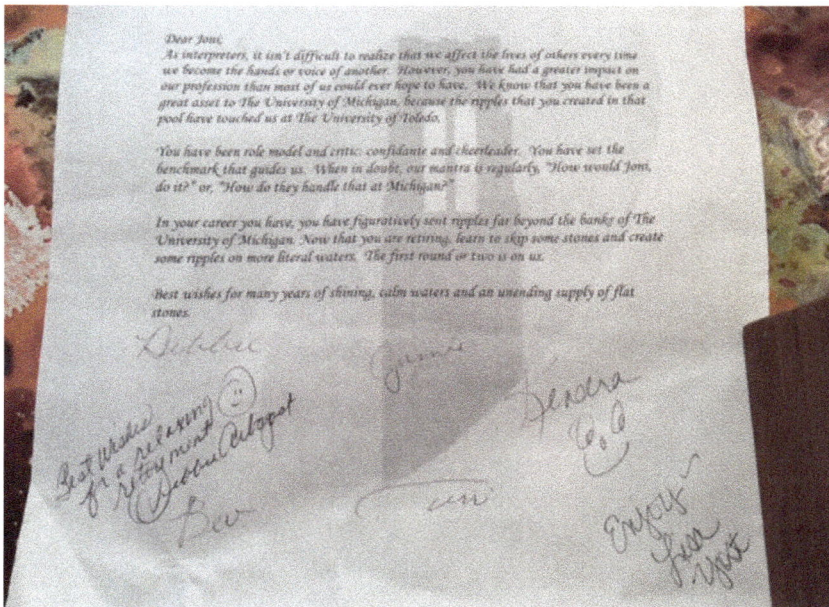

"efforts must come from the present generation, especially young people, with confidence and hope and activation of our potential" (see Photo 2).

His Holiness Tenzin Gyatso, Fourteenth Dalai Lama and spiritual and secular leader of the Tibetan people, is revered by Tibetans and Buddhists worldwide. Since 1959 he has lived in exile in India and struggled to resolve his country's political problems peacefully, while protecting and enhancing the Tibetan culture and language. In 1989 he was awarded the Nobel Peace Prize.

Edward (Ed) Loyer, the First Council Chair

Assistant University Registrar **Edward Clark Loyer** died Sept. 27 after a short illness. He was 68.

Loyer (Photo courtesy Loyer family)

Loyer was a man of many interests and talents, including being an avid cyclist, jazz enthusiast, and passionate supporter of the arts and theatre. He saw himself as an administrator/educator with an emphasis on educator.

Loyer was born in Belding Mich., the son of Vance and Mildred Loyer. He graduated from Ohio University in 1961 with degrees in business and theater and began his career with Univac in 1962, working with first-generation computers. In 1966 he joined U-M in the Data Systems Center and soon moved to the Registrar's Office, where he was director of records and transcripts for 30 years. The last 10 years he taught in the Michigan Administrative Information Services Student Information Systems.

Loyer was active in the life of the University and Ann Arbor community, including mentoring hundreds of Evans Scholars in the 24 years he served as faculty advisor to the group. He served as the chairman of the Council for Disability Concerns and president of the Board of Governors of the Michigan League. He also was a member of the Campus Safety and Security Advisory Committee and on the board of the Ann Arbor Center for Independent Living. He also was a trustee at the First Congregational Church of Ann Arbor, where he taught church school.

While he was very proud of his association with U-M, he equally was proud of the 33 years he taught data processing at Washtenaw Community College.

Active in his profession, Loyer served on several committees of the American Association of Collegiate Registrars and Admission Officers. At the state level, he was president of the Michigan Association of Collegiate Registrars and Admission Officers and for many years was newsletter editor. Loyer was remembered with a video tribute Nov. 3

when some 300 colleagues from across the state gathered in Lansing for the association's 77th annual conference.

Family and friends gathered Oct. 1 at the First Congregational Church to celebrate his life. They recall Loyer as a rare individual that everyone liked and he always was the center of attention—but the attention never was on him. His favorite quote came from Mary Chase's play "Harvey": *"In this world, you must be oh so smart or oh so pleasant. Well, for years I was smart. I recommend pleasant."*

Loyer is survived by his wife, Sandra Aiken Loyer, to whom he was married for 43 years; three sons, Chris of Irvine Calif., Tim (Christine) of Chicago, and Josh and partner Mary Murphrey of Ann Arbor; and a sister, Martha Basile of Rocky River, Ohio.

Memorial contributions may be made to the Evans Scholar Foundation, Ann Arbor Center for Independent Living or First Congregational Church of Ann Arbor.

—Submitted by Paul Wright, Registrar's Office. Source University Record 1/3/2006

Photo 2 Photo from "Ann Arbor News" of Joan E. Smith and His Holiness after Joan "signed" for his presentation at the Wallenberg Lecture on April 21, 1994

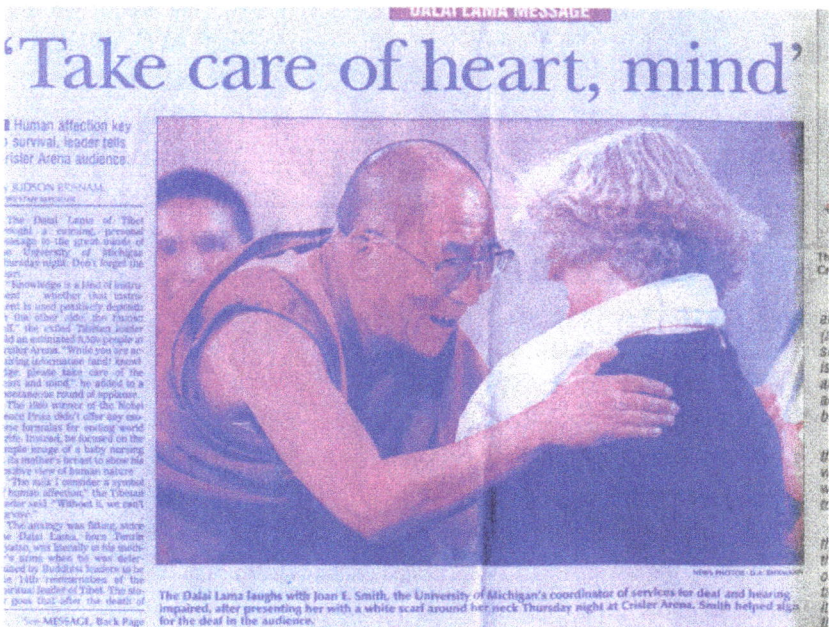

'Take care of heart, mind'

This anecdote that was told about Ed Loyer may be apocryphal but, nevertheless, since it is a pleasant one to contemplate and seems to indicate his philosophy, it would be remiss to leave it out in this history: It was reported that he decided, after many, many years of being surrounded by many learned, intelligent individuals in the halls of academe, that "it is much better to be nice than to be smart."

Joan E. Smith (Joni), the recipient of the second ever James T. Neubacher Award, wrote this description about the first-ever Council Chair Edward (Ed) Loyer on the day he announced to her that she was the Neubacher awardee:

> Ed Loyer came across campus on his bicycle, wearing a sports coat, hat and smoking a pipe. He waved an arm to call me over. He started with the pronouncement of The Neubacher Award, ME? My amazement was obvious, as he began listing the reasons why. How could they possibly know about all those things? He continued to surprise me with his long list of activities in the field of Disability. His involvement with the Center for Independent Living as a volunteer and motivational speaker benefitted many of their participants. The university recognized his extra abilities by engaging him for different speaker roles at varying events. The best ones were duo presentations with his charming wife, Sandra Loyer. His funeral was so packed, people were in the waiting room. Every time you interacted with Ed Loyer, you came away a better person. His work and leadership on The Council for Disability Concerns was the start of a wave of good and concerned members of the University, lasting into 2017.

Typical Topics in Early Council Meeting Discussions (Culled from a Collection of 1999 Minutes)

The members were concerned about a multitude of topics including recruitment and employment of persons with disabilities along with gauging how the university is perceived as an employer; students with psychiatric disabilities; graduate students with disabilities; need for test taking accommodations along with ergonomics; attitudinal issues of supervisors; national leadership and networking on issues related to students with disabilities; disability as part of a Living/Learning curriculum; evacuation procedures for people with disabilities; benefits of universal design principles in all campus planning; departmental/school advocacy; marginalization of students; marketing of council to be included in university of mission; housing and adjustment to dorm living (peer training Resident Assistants); collaborating with University Musical Society on events that bring in performer with disabilities; inviting Flint and Dearborn campuses to be involved; counseling services for area of learning disabilities; student pressure to "conform to the norm"; planning for

Investing in Abilities Week; budgetary concerns with possibilities for funding; disability attitudes in other cultures; international possibilities of exchange.

The James Edward Knox Center is named after Jim Knox (1944–2010), the first director of the first U-M adaptive technology computing site. Jim (see Photo 3) became interested in computer accommodations in the mid-1980s when a blind student, A. Douglas Thompson, inquired why he had to pay fees each semester to use computer equipment that was inaccessible to him. Together, Jim and Doug established the Barrier-Free Computer User Group, which met regularly to learn about assistive technology options and advocate for improved accessibility.

- Over time, Jim worked tirelessly to develop assistive technology initiatives at U-M. Besides providing one-on-one assistance to U-M community members, he helped develop the Ergopod, an innovative accessible workstation, and Talking Points (http://ns.umich.edu/new/releases/6737), a Bluetooth-based orientation system. He co-authored papers for a number of major assistive technology conferences and was acknowledged as an authority on assistive technology in university environments.
- Jim had a passion for good food, classical music, nature, travel, literature and sports. His gregariousness was as legendary as his kindness. He inspired loyalty and affection throughout U-M, and the re-naming of his cherished computer lab ensures that his legacy will endure.
- One of the university's first computer whiz kids, Jim was invited to teach at Harvard University after he and a fellow graduate co-authored

Photo 3 James Edward Knox

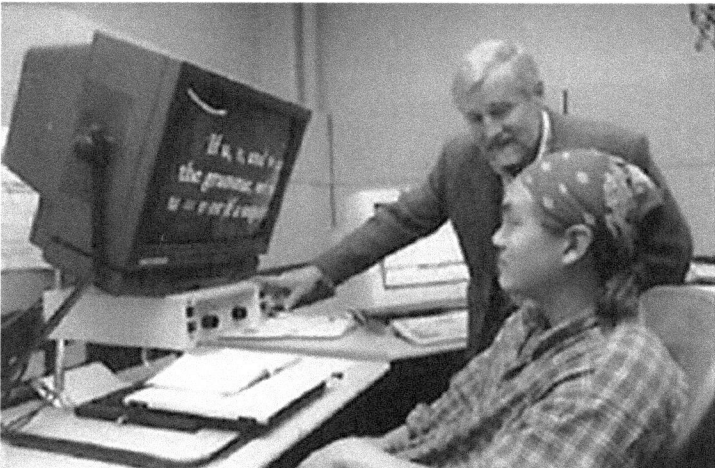

a paper on the first computer-oriented graphical geographic information system (GIS). Jim stayed in Ann Arbor and worked for the University of Michigan for more than thirty years. In the mid 1980's, in addition to working as Postmaster/ Ombudsman/User Advocate for Information Technology Services, he established the adaptive technology computing site (ATCS) in the Shapiro Undergraduate Library where students, staff, and faculty with spinal cord injuries, visual and hearing impairments, dyslexia, carpal tunnel syndrome, and other disabilities have access to adaptive hardware, software and workstations. He even helped design special needs computer workstations . . . Countless students have credited him with their academic success."— *Annarbor.com obituary, July 8, 2010* (http://obits.mlive.com/obituaries/annarbor/obituary.aspx?n=jim-knox&pid=143971626)

- In a very unsung and understated way, he was always working to help folks with disabilities be better able to use computing technology. That was a big passion for Jim. He also believed in computing overall and wanted to keep the computing environment safe and friendly for everyone so that all could benefit from the positive things it has to offer. He was one of the rocks of simple, positive practice on which the U-M computing community was built over the years.

- One can't really appreciate that kind of contribution enough until you travel to other campuses where you see a more convoluted, locked-down, dysfunctional computing environment. It makes all the difference in the world in your daily work, and our system was born from a caring philosophy about people and a dedication to work through the hard problems so users wouldn't have to. Jim wasn't the only one, but he was right there on the front lines, never giving up, always advocating for the user against unnecessary bureaucracy, restraints or obfuscation. And he gained a very positive reputation in the IT community for these efforts.—*John Cady, U-M colleague, A Man of Michigan* (http://www-personal .umich.edu/~bing/jimknox/Jim_Knox.html)

Nowadays, the Knox Center is coordinated by Jane Vincent-Berliss with the assistance of Brandon Werner. The staff members have made substantial improvements on the original unit, increasing both its size and technological capacities. As the description on the website says,

The Knox Center meets the needs of U-M community members, primarily students, who have questions about modifications or alternatives to standard monitors, keyboards or mice, or who are seeking high-tech tools to help with reading and writing.

Specialized hardware and software are provided at multiple Windows and Macintosh computers, all of which have 21″ or larger high-resolution monitors. All workstations also have adjustable-height work surfaces to accommodate wheelchairs or people who wish to stand. One reclining chair is available, and the other chairs are fully adjustable. One workstation has a video magnifier. There is a set of lockers to temporarily store your belongings if you wish; please bring your own lock.

Room 2064A (see Photo 4) within the Knox Center has three computers with voice recognition software: two Windows machines running Dragon NaturallySpeaking and one Mac running Dragon for Mac. Priority for use of this room will be given first to Knox Center staff who are doing evaluations and second to individuals using the Dragon programs. The Knox Center is designated as quiet space. We appreciate everyone's help in maintaining this. (http://its.umich.edu/computing/accessible-computing/atcs/about)

Photo 4 Room 2064A within the Knox Center

Current Council Organization and Membership (2017)

Currently chaired by the Intellectual Property Attorney in the U-M Office of the president and coordinated by the Disabilities/Diversity/Outreach Librarian, council membership is open to everyone, both U-M-affiliates and members of the local community. It includes a number of staff members from SSD, such as the Director and the Coordinator for the Deaf and Hard of Hearing; a number of librarians; hospital revenue sharing staff; the University Accessibility Webmaster; and the ADA Coordinator. Other members come from the Institute for Social Research; the Collegiate Recovery Program (CRP), the School of Nursing; University |Admissions; the Office of Institutional Equity (OIE); the School of Engineering; the Plant Department; as well as some University Information Technology units. Included as members are a variety of information technology and adaptive technology experts, representatives from the University Health System (Michigan Medicine) and the Medical School, and a large group of interested individuals from the local community. There are representatives from the Ann Arbor Center for Independent Living and also from the City of Ann Arbor Commission on Disability Issues. Some of the members have visible disabilities and others do not. Some of the members declare their disability and others do not. The only requirement for membership is interest in belonging to the council.

Whereas the monthly meetings are usually attended by up to twenty or thirty people, the council also has a mailing list of approximately three hundred individuals to whom meeting minutes and other communications are sent on a regular basis. There are also a U-M Regent and several former Regents on the mailing list. Almost one hundred of these council members are non-U-M-affiliates, including several from other countries. The council's services to the university are acknowledged and welcomed by the university as well as by the members of the local community. The council members' ultimate goal is to collaborate with similar organizations, and thus to create a global platform for the council's vision while providing an example as well as ideas for its implementation.

The workload of each meeting is distributed because the council is coordinated by one individual and chaired by another. Notifications of upcoming meetings and minutes of past meetings are distributed by email to members by the coordinator, including interesting news reports or relevant articles about new technology and disability issues, along with upcoming university or community events. The monthly meetings of the council are characterized by lively and relatively informal discussions. There is often an invited presenter on subjects ranging from special "apps" for people with chronic disease, to psychiatric implications of disability, to three-dimensional maps of the campus, along with numerous other topics and themes of interest. Previous presenters have included young entrepreneurs interested in accessible designing for the disabled community, engineering students whose assignment was to create an example of adaptive technology, a team from the Hospital's Department of Physical Medicine and Rehabilitation reporting on their project about preparing disabled youth for the job market, a medical student describing her work with children in the cancer center, the organizer of a division of personal assistants, and many others. Meetings are held in an available venue that is large enough to hold the number of members expected to attend and that is accessible for wheelchair users. Recently, remote access through Skype and BlueJeans also became available. New members are always welcome, and the council members emphasize an enthusiastic outreach effort to anyone interested in joining, including members of the U-M Dearborn and U-M Flint campuses.

The Website of the CFDC

The council's website (ability.umich.edu) is the repository for its activities, history, recent monthly meeting minutes, and links to such relevant resources as "Accommodating Employees with Psychiatric Disabilities," "U-M Occupational Health Services" (with its informational flyer on for changes in ability to work), "Campus Mind Works" (relevant student mental health issues), and "Accessible Website Information." Since the council has now acquired a dedicated webmaster, the information contained in the website can change whenever an addition or correction has to be made to the contents. A calendar of events is in the planning stages to alert council members to programs of possible interest. In addition, there is a schedule of Investing in Ability events, which address a different theme every October. Included on the website are the biographies of Award recipients as well as several recordings of the James T. Neubacher Awards Ceremony.

Accomplishments in Recent Years

As a specific example of an instance of council support, on one occasion the members provided assistance and a referral for an individual who was frustrated by and wanted to address a medical situation in which a baby with a disability was born, and the medical caregivers seemed to disparage the newborn because of its condition. Although not actually a council member, this individual came to a meeting for advice and subsequently received a connection with a program in a medical school to educate and sensitize medical students early in their careers. The individual went on to serve as a liaison and advocate for newborns to staff members of other institutions.

In another collaborative affirmation of council's enthusiasm in raising the profile of the broad spectrum of disabilities, the members were delighted to acknowledge a new council member, a professor who represents autism/Asperger's syndrome in a very personal way at conferences, through lectures, social media, and publications, all communications that, the council members believe, will make a difference to many by encouraging others with similar conditions to feel welcome in our community and in the larger world as well.

Occasionally, a professor assigns a class a project that turns out to be very useful to the cause of accessibility/disability on campus. One outstanding example was a social experiment to raise consciousness about accessibility, an assignment that resulted in a video, one that was posted to YouTube. The students assigned classmates, as an experiment, to navigate the campus for a day, attending all their classes without climbing any stairs, as if they were all wheelchair users (https://www.youtube.com/watch?v=LP1L_mAWzDQ).

Bridging the Chasm between the Central and the U-M Medical Campuses

A little known historical fact is that the council members from Central Campus in the early years of the twenty-first century took particular pride in the fact that they were campus pioneers in welcoming and collaborating with members from the U-M Health System community and thus forming a bridge across the chasm between the two campuses, at the time an uncommon occurrence. It was discovered that a number of staff members in the Medical Center considered themselves strictly U-M Hospital employees rather than members of the University of Michigan community. Fortunately, in the mid-1990s, a very dynamic Human Resources diversity coordinator from the Health System by the name of Cathy Frank encouraged and initially provided the connection between campuses. The bond became stronger over the years to the point that nobody recalls that this harmonious collaboration between members of these two major divisions had seldom been noted in a similar committee at the university previously. Diversity somehow morphed into disability as the campuses merged in the council. Furthermore, Cathy served as a sort of fairy godmother to the council because just before retiring, she introduced the council to Craig Luck and vice versa. Craig, the manager for the food/vending and valet parking contracts at the U-M Hospital, joined the membership and has been an invaluable partner in council activities ever since, in particular with the James T. Neubacher Award Ceremony. He has helped to make it a successful, happy event for over a decade. Not to be forgotten is another amazing recruit from the

Medical Campus at that time, Gerald Hoff, the originator and organizer of the eagerly awaited annual Army-Navy Wheelchair Games, a celebratory sports event held every year since 2006.

Major Events Organized and Promoted by the Council

The CFDC sponsors two major events during the academic year: the James T. Neubacher Award and Investing in Ability. The Neubacher Award is a one-time annual recognition ceremony, whereas the Investing in Ability program has grown to encompass a wide range of disability-related activities and awareness-building events. Although originally limited to the span of only one week during the month of October, the scope and number of Investing in Ability events have expanded to cover almost the whole month and even occasionally extend into November.

The James T. Neubacher Award

At the end of October, the James T. Neubacher Award is presented to an individual or team connected with the university who has made a significant contribution to disability rights. The council selected the month of October to coincide with the state of Michigan's observance of Investing in Ability. The purpose of this special observance is to promote employment of people with disabilities by encouraging employers as well as to encourage the general public to focus on a person's abilities rather than his or her disabilities. At the Ceremony, a special plaque and a sum of money from the President's Office are given in honor of Jim Neubacher, an alumnus of the university, who was a columnist for *The Detroit Free Press* and an advocate for equal rights and opportunities for people with disabilities. Through the years, recipients of the Award have ranged from students to staff members to faculty to alumni. In addition, a number of Certificates of Appreciation are handed out at the ceremony in recognition of university-affiliated individuals or teams who have worked to destigmatize disability and raise consciousness about accessibility. The ceremony is an uplifting celebratory one with up to twenty or twenty-five certificates distributed and friends, families, and colleagues gathered in the audience to enjoy the food, company, and recognition of the award and certificate recipients.

> **The Neubacher and Me** (informal notes about the logistics of the Neubacher Awards written in 2008 by the Chair of James T. Neubacher Award Committee, 2004–2017):

> This is my thirteenth year to chair the University of Michigan's annual Neubacher Award Committee, and while I am not suggesting

that with practice, I perform better in this position every year, I do feel that I have had sufficient experience to be able to write about it. The flattering part is to be nominated to chair the committee, and then the work begins. First, we find five volunteers from the Council for Disability Concerns, either from the University or from the community. Then, we immediately decide what our final date will be for accepting nominations and when we can all meet to discuss them. After that, there is something of a peaceful hiatus wherein I collaborate and communicate with Human Resources to get the website and the publicity flyers ready for distribution. When the cards have been printed, there is also the process of targeted e-mail that is sent out to everyone on campus, which is interesting, because one cannot imagine how many "out of office" replies are generated by this activity—and they all come back to me as the sender. As the day of the deadline approaches, there is sometimes a little flurry of panic exhibited by nominators who wonder whether it is too late. My reply is always that it is never too late. I have sent a response to each nominator, thanking him or her for his or her interest in our enterprise. On the day of decision, the committee of 6 or 7 members convenes. We each have copies of all the nominations, which I have already forwarded to everyone in the group, and we have made lists of our top fifteen or twenty candidates, depending on how many forms were submitted. If a decision cannot be made at that first meeting, and it usually cannot, we set a date for another meeting. At the following meeting (or meetings, if need be), we come to our final decision, leaving the other top contenders to be awarded a Certificate of Appreciation. Next, I notify the recipients of all the awards, and we proceed to plan the event itself. We invite the awardees, their nominators, a number of deans, department heads, and faculty members who may be interested in attending the Ceremony, as well as a contingent of University leaders. I have already invited a University member, either a Regent or someone else in a high U-M leadership position, to present the plaque for the Neubacher Award after introducing the recipient. The arrangements that have to be put in place for the event consist of the plaque for the recipient of the major award, a reception table with name tags and programs, appropriate seating and layout that is considerate of wheelchair users, Communication Access Realtime Translation (CART), transcribed screen writing for the deaf and hard of hearing); the Continental breakfast for all attendees; and the lunch for the Neubacher recipient, the committee members, and a number of selected individuals. I always wish that we could invite the entire audience to lunch, something that, unfortunately, we cannot afford to do.

The Council Chair, Jack Bernard, opens the ceremony, usually but not always humorously; and I, as Coordinator, follow his lead with my descriptions, which I compose in advance, listing the activities that earned each recipient a Certificate of Appreciation. (One year, the entire ceremony was videotaped by a unit called Campus Automated Rich Media Archiving (CARMA), thanks to some extra funding given us by our Human Resources Vice-President Laurita Thomas.) The final part of the event consists of awarding the Neubacher plaque (to be followed later by a sum of money from the President's Office) and a little talk or possibly a video presentation by the recipient. After this, a section of the participants, including the Award recipient and the person(s) who nominated him or her, plus other guests, adjourn to lunch and socialize.

From this activity, I have learned to hone my organizational skills, to improve my personal skills by making sure that I reach out to all in a friendly fashion, to sharpen my memory skills by remembering to send reminders, to brighten up my attitude by looking on the positive side of people (there are often so many positive sides if one looks), and to be as succinct and efficient as possible while still maintaining an enthusiastic personal style to bring out the fact that the University of Michigan has great people doing great things for others (see Photo 5).

Photo 5 2008 James T. Neubacher Award Ceremony Program

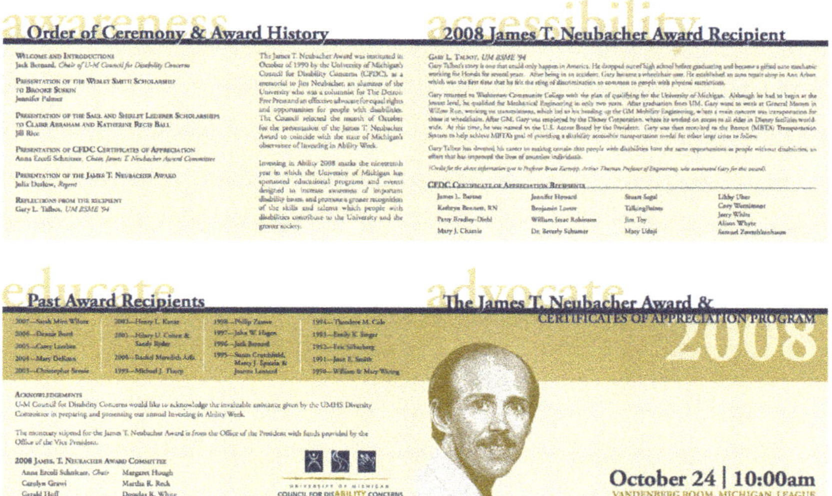

A Typical Neubacher Award Recipient (if there is such a person since they are all so diverse):

Gary L. Talbot was recognized for his achievements in the area of disabilities at the 2008 University of Michigan Neubacher Award Ceremony. As you will note, he himself suffered a serious injury years ago that resulted in his becoming a wheelchair user; however, he turned this seeming physical misfortune into an opportunity to provide access to others, in particular to other wheelchair users. He is now known for using his skills acquired in engineering in conjunction with his empathy for others who had special needs—to facilitate transportation access not only in the City of Boston's (MBTA) Metropolitan Boston's Transportation Authority but also in our very own city of Ann Arbor, as Amtrak's current ADA Program Director, where he created Amtrak's first technologically advanced station platform facilitating onboarding for all.

Gary Talbot's story is one that could only happen in America. He dropped out of high school before graduating and became a gifted auto mechanic working for Honda for several years. After being in an accident, Gary became a wheelchair user. He established an auto repair shop in Ann Arbor, which was the first time that he felt the sting of discrimination so common to people with physical restrictions.

Gary returned to Washtenaw Community College with the plan of qualifying for the University of Michigan. Although he had to begin at the lowest level, he qualified for Mechanical Engineering in only two years. After graduation from U-M, Gary went to work at General Motors in Willow Run, working on transmissions, which led to his heading up the GM Mobility Engineering, where a main concern was transportation for those in wheelchairs. After GM, Gary was employed by the Disney Corporation, where he worked on access to all rides in Disney facilities worldwide.

At this time, he was named to the US Access Board by the President. Gary was then recruited to the Boston (MBTA) to help achieve the goal of providing a disability accessible transportation model for other large cities to follow.

Gary Talbot has devoted his career to making certain that people with disabilities have the same opportunities as people without disabilities, an effort that has improved the lives of countless individuals. (Except for the introductory paragraph, credit for the above information goes to Professor Bruce Karnopp, Arthur Thurnau Professor of Engineering, who nominated Gary for the U-M's 2008 James T. Neubacher Award.)

To watch a recording of the 2008 Neubacher Award Ceremony, please visit https://lib.mivideo.it.umich.edu/media/2008+James+T.+Neubacher+Award+Ceremony/1_2x5pl12c.

Years later, Gary Talbot returned to Ann Arbor, and in his current capacity of Amtrak Disability Consultant, he engineered new technology for accessible travel in creating a platform at the Ann Arbor Amtrak Station to bridge the gap between the platform and the train, with ergonomic design making the operation easy for employees and safer for passengers, both with and without disabilities (see Photo 6). Gary Talbot stated, "Our goal is to ensure that stations for which Amtrak has ADA responsibility are accessible to all passengers."

List of (recent) James T. Neubacher Award Recipients:

- Robert Adams, 2017, Chair of UMInDS/U-M professor
- Cooper Charlton, 2016, U-M graduate/student body president
- Eric Hipple, 2015, staff member, U-M Depression Center
- Lloyd Shelton, 2014, staff member, U-M SSD
- John Greden, MD, 2013, faculty member, U-M Depression Center
- Samuel Bagenstos, 2012, faculty member, U-M School of Law
- Richard Bernstein, 2011, Attorney/Disability Advocate
- Barbara Kornblau, 2010, Dean of Health Professions, U-M Flint
- Tobin Siebers, 2009, Chair of UMInDS/U-M Professor

List of (more recent) annual October Investing in Ability themes:

- Stigma, Stereotypes, and Bullying
- Diversity Includes Disability

Photo 6 Ann Arbor Amtrak Platform, first in Michigan

Source: CNN story about Gary Talbot: http://www.cnn.com/2010/LIVING/07/26/ada.talbot/

- Substance Abuse ("Is Addiction a Disability?")
- Invisible Disabilities (Hidden Stories)
- HonorABLE: Honoring our Veterans
- Art and Architecture of Accessibility
- Maximizing Your Ability throughout Life (with Prof. Christopher Peterson)

List of (more recent) U-M Accomplishments (and recent Hires) regarding Disability:

- Knox Center & Coordinator
- LSA Testing Accommodation Center & Coordinator
- Accessibility Webmaster and Screen Reader Positions
- HathiTrust Digital Library (totally searchable access for SSD enrollees)
- Annual U-M Army-Navy Wheelchair Basketball Game
- Wording about accommodations offered in acceptance letters to students

Opportunities for U-M to be the Leaders and Best in Providing a Disability-Friendly Campus (a Wish-List):

- Increasing campus awareness of currently available assistance and accommodations
- Surveying campus to identify any unmet special needs
- Fulfilling unmet special needs for accommodation, transportation, and special assistance through both increased staffing and funding
- Continuing to reach out and admit students with disabilities as an important part of our U-M Diversity Initiative

Events Held during the Council's Investing in Ability Series

The Army-Navy Wheelchair Basketball Game

As a very festive, celebratory part of our annual Investing in Ability program, usually scheduled as the final event, every fall since 2009 the council has presented a Wheelchair Basketball Game (see Photos 7 and 8). This sports event started out very humbly in the local high school gym with few spectators and not much fanfare; however, every year it becomes more well attended and well known with additional attractions and a larger, more enthusiastic audience, having developed into a well-loved standard.

All due credit for this exciting event goes to Gerald Hoff who has initiated and organized this annual event and who has worked to inspire more and more participants every year. The purpose of the game is to honor veterans, both student-veterans and others in the community, as well as inviting people with physical challenges and providing a showcase for the skills of our wheelchair athletes. The U-M Dance Team takes part along with the U-M Cheerleader Team and the U-M Tri-Service Color Guard. The 338th Army Band plays and there is additional appropriate marching music. The Honorary Marshalls through the years have included such dignitaries as Congressman John Dingell, Ron Warhurst, Robert McDivitt, Mike Lantry, and Ted Spencer. The players have included Paralympian Paul Schulte and numerous other athletes, both expert and new wheelchair users.

Photo 7 Scenes from Army-Navy Wheelchair Games held in U-M's Crisler Arena

2010 UM ARMY-NAVY WHEELCHAIR BASKETBALL GAME.

The motorcade ran from the Michigan Union to Saline High. The game wa played on a Friday and at 5:30 PM we had State street totally shut down t allow our motorcade to run nonstop through every intersection/lights to the game.

The 2010th Battalion used 6 Humvees, we also had multiple Sheriff's vehicles that escorted our UM buses to the game.

(Continued)

(Continued)

Gerald Hoff shared his photo.
October 12 at 4:12am · 🌐

···

Navy coach CAPT Joe H. Evans, USN

The red hot sharp shooting 2014 UM Navy Team!

The two players in the back row on the far right are current UM SVA President USMC Jon Medicelli and former UM SVA President USMC Will Kerkstra. Don't be fooled by their smile, these two guys are flat out tenacious competitors.

2010 Game Army won 52-49 - 2011 Game Navy won 36-34 - 2012 Game Navy won 32-27 - 2013 Game Navy won 31-22 - 2014 Game Navy won 44-37 — with Jody Talbott, Joshua Simister, Jimmy Moceri, Bryan Richar, Roy Berg, Ben Creekmore, Jon Mendicelli and William Kerkstra.

Gerald Hoff is with William Kerkstra and 8 others.
July 21, 2015 · 👥

Navy coach CAPT Joe H. Evans, USN

The red hot sharp shooting 2014 UM Navy Team!

UM Army-Navy Wheelchair Basketball Game.
Paul-Meg Schulte with Mo Phillips Jr and Jesus Villa

Photo 8 Visitors at the Army-Navy Wheelchair Game, 2016, an Investing in Ability event

(Continued)

(Continued)

Myreo Dixon (left), Mark Appleton (right), Lillian Strother (center), 5 years old.

Because of the popularity of the Council's Army-Navy Wheelchair Game, an additional wheelchair game was held at Saline High School Auditorium in Saline, Michigan, in 2016, by special request of their teachers and students. The Detroit Diehard team members and other wheelchair champions are seen in the front row with US Naval officers behind them. Future games may also be held at Dexter Schools and at Eastern Michigan University (see Photo 9).

Selection of Some of the Keynote Speakers at Earlier Investing in Ability Events

John Hockenberry, NBC news correspondent, two-time Peabody Award Winner, paraplegic since auto accident at age 19.

Richard Pimental, nationally known speaker on disability management, worker's compensation, rehabilitation, cost containment and

Photo 9 Wheelchair game held at Saline High School Auditorium in Saline, Michigan

interpersonal relationships in the workplace; lost hearing during the Vietnam War and developed tinnitus as a result.

Chris "Crazy Legs" Fonseca, comedian who has cerebral palsy.

Victor J. Strecher, speaker/author of "On Purpose: Lessons in Life and Health from the Frog and the Dung Beetle," deeply affected by loss of his daughter to heart disease.

Paul Coehlo, US Congressman and chief architect of the ADA federal legislation passed in 1990, consciousness about disability raised by a fall that caused his epilepsy.

Richard Bernstein, Michigan Justice of the Supreme Court, born visually impaired.

Service Animals and Therapy Dogs Invited during Investing in Ability

One big event, originally held in an open space called "The Diag" in front of the Graduate Library every October as part of the annual Investing in Ability series, brings together dogs to campus for the purpose of destigmatizing disability in a positive way while focusing on the animal-human bond and the assistance dogs can provide regarding accessibility to daily activities (see Photos 10–13). Additional venues for dog viewing had to be set up in view of the popularity of the "Dogs in the Diag." The hospital itself, the hospital's billing arm, another medical campus, and yet another campus location just north of central campus were selected as places where the dogs could be seen (and patted). There are a number of reasons for this gathering: first, everyone seems to be attracted by it and it serves as a "kick-off" to the rest of our program; second, it is educational for students in a gentle, consciousness-raising way; third, it allows the dogs to become accustomed to a crowded yet friendly situation; and, last but far from least, everybody loves the dogs.

Photo 10 Group of human and canine members of Paws with a Cause at an early "Dogs in the Diag" campus event established to serve as a "kick-off" for Investing in Ability. Mary Blain is Paws Coordinator (in center) with support group and their charges

Photo 11 The "Dogs in the Diag" all started over a dozen years ago with the original service dog Ukon belonging to Council member Jane MacFarlane. After Jane introduced the Council to Paws with a Cause, the "Dogs in the Diag" event evolved and grew exponentially from that early introduction

Photo 12 Jane and Ukon are both gone now, but as can be observed in this slightly edited Facebook posting, far from forgotten

November 12 at 11:38am · Edited · 🌐 ▾

Jane was proud of her friendship with Anna Ercoli Schnitzer and her affiliation with the University of Michigan's Council on Disability Concerns. As a result of this friendship, "Dogs on the Diag" was launched in 2005, to bring awareness to faculty and students during "Investing in Abilities Week" of the important role that Assistance Dogs play in the lives of their owners. Many foster puppy raisers and clients have participated in this event since that time.

This year Paws With A Cause received a Certificate of Appreciation from the Council. Jane MacFarlane, you and Ukon were the heart of this event from the beginning

Photo 13 Spencer Steff, another dog lover at the Dogs on the Diag event in 2008

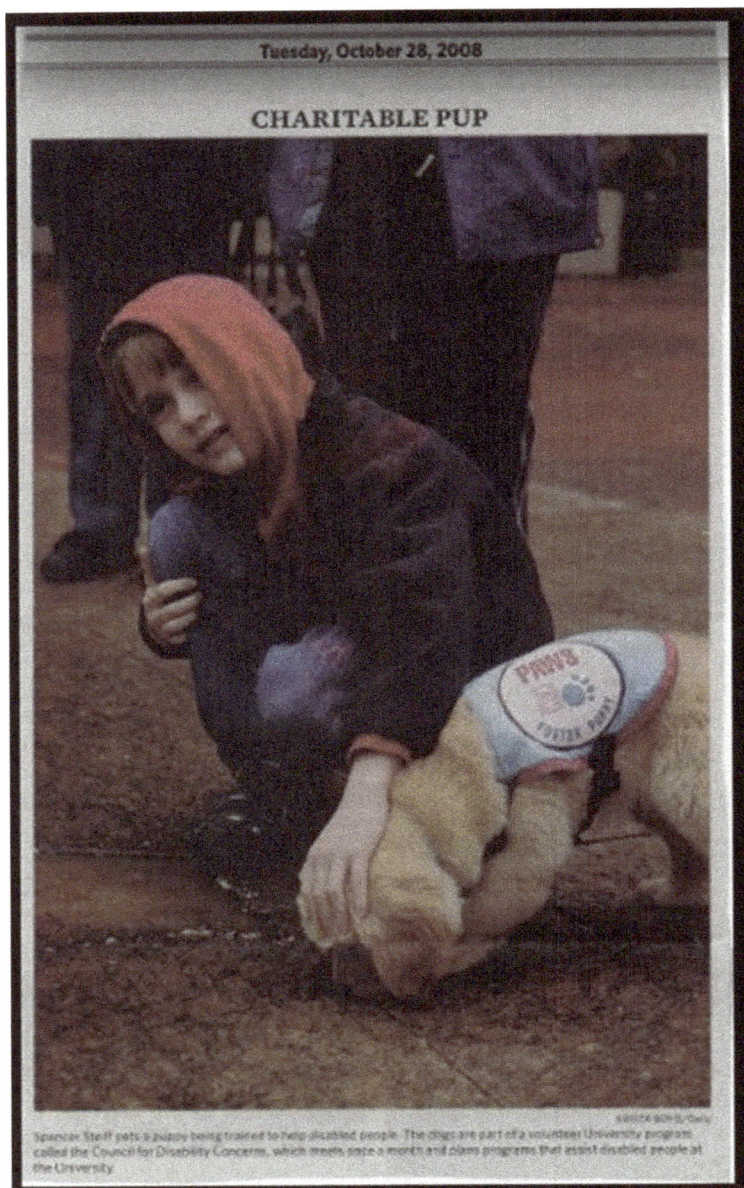

Tuesday, October 28, 2008

CHARITABLE PUP

Spencer Steff pets a puppy being trained to help disabled people. The dogs are part of a volunteer University program called the Council for Disability Concerns, which meets once a month and plans programs that assist disabled people at the University.

The Council and the Community

One of our long-time loyal council members Dr. Els R. Nieuwenhuijsen Eldersveld, a pioneer in disability studies on campus and elsewhere, has written a paper that helps bring the reader up to date on disability awareness with respect to the University of Michigan and the surrounding community (see Photo 14). In her discussion titled "Status of Disability Awareness and Related Activities at the U-M and the Community," she writes, "These notes and observations are compiled as background for an initiative to the U-M gift-giving department to make some kind of contribution to bridge the gap between U-M and the community."

Photo 14 Excerpts from Dr. Els R. Nieuwenhuijsen Eldersveld's paper

Status of disability awareness and related activities at the U-M and community

Els R. Nieuwenhuijsen Eldersveld, PhD, MPH, OTR/retired

Rough draft May 2, 2017

Introduction

These notes and observations are compiled as background for an initiative to the UM gift -giving dept. to make some kind of contribution to bridge the gap between U-M and the community. I reflect on the status of disability awareness and related actions within the U-M and the AA community, by exploring 3 questions: 1. What is the status of awareness of disability at the U-M? 2. How is the term disability used (defined)? 3. The gap between U-M disability-related actions and the community, and why this is of concern (*still in development*). The term disability in this paper is grounded on the intersection/interaction between a person with a (physical or mental) health condition and his/her environmental barriers. This concept is based on the bio-psycho-social model of disability as described by the International Classification of Functioning, Disability and Health (WHO 2001). This paper is a work in progress..

1. *What is the status of awareness of disability at the U-M?*
    To answer this question I looked at (a) the progress made by the U-M Council for Disability Concerns (CfDC) in terms of disability-related awareness on campus (I am a member of the CfDC since 1992; (b) the status of teaching disability at graduate and/or undergraduate level at the U-M; (c) disability related policies (in process). In-depth research in answering these questions is beyond the scope of this paper.

    In 2003 a survey took place among Council stakeholders (N=?) to identify issues and challenges facing people with disability at the U-M, and to develop a systematic approach to overcome and identify environmental barriers. The results of this survey were presented in a strategic plan, which consisted of 2 broad objectives:
    1. Increase (disability) awareness and education of the general University community, and the University leadership,
    2. Promote consistent University disability policy interpretation.
    Significant progress has been made in particular by the (educational and other) activities coordinated by the CfDC since 2003.
    - The CfDC meetings are currently very well attended by a growing number of students and staff with and without disability, representing different disciplines (e.g., *include the number of CfDC members using the e-mail list, and include a table with the list of departments representing monthly meetings?*).

1

2. How is the term disability used?

The 2nd broad CfDC strategic objective identified in 2013 is "to promote consistent University disability policy interpretation". This objective is important not only for policy but also for communication, data collection, comparison of research. But also for education, eliminating stigma, identification and removing of environmental barriers. More evaluation is necessary to collect examples. However, a quick review of the application of the term disability leads to the following discovery. First, the term disability is widely used most likely because of the Americans With Disabilities Act (1990). The conceptual framework of disability used at U-M is inconsistent. The Services for Students with Disabilities (SSDS) website refers to a wide range of diagnostic groups as well as some categories related to impairments. The Center for Population Studies defines disability as "difficulties with activities of daily living". The Department of PM&R mission and purpose is to "develop effective solutions to maximize health, function, and quality of life of people with physical and cognitive disability across the lifespan....". UmINDS views disability as a "political construction and cultural identity, not simply as a medical condition. Disability is not only a set of physical or mental differences but the product of interactions between physical, cultural, and political environments shaping the perception and experience of different capacities".

Recommendations for future CfDC Investing in Abilities Week themes and activities:

- What is a disability-friendly campus? Strategies to strengthen accessibility and inclusion.
- Discuss the indicators of the best accessible America cities (see attached). Are these indicators useful to transform UM North campus in a disability friendly campus (see the draft of January 2007).
- Roundtable discussions about the meaning of disability, building on the international framework, under the leadership of CRLT
- A symposium: past, present, and future of disability in Ann Arbor: presentations by UM scholars and community representatives and roundtable discussions.

3

Retiring ADA Coordinator Carole Dubritsky (Her Retiring Interview Transcribed)

At her final meeting before retiring from her position at the university, on January 28, 2016, ADA Coordinator Carole Dubritsky of OIE gave a farewell address to the CFDC at a monthly meeting sharing the many issues and experiences she has encountered over the years as U-M's ADA Coordinator. (For this final presentation at the council by Carole and the remarks that followed, recording is available at https://drive.google .com/file/d/0By-lfENntcBNQ0NXNURhekQ4YVE/view?usp=sharing.) After a glowing introduction by Council Chair Jack Bernard describing how our ADA Coordinator changed the university for the better through her actions, Carole Dubritsky reminisces about her dozen years in her position, although she had been active doing disability work even before she was officially appointed to the U-M Office of Institutional Equity. Carole stated that her job was "the best job on campus, and the hardest job on campus because it is a moving target and one never knows what is coming down the road." She describes how complex the campus is and how large and spread out, with over 350 buildings constructed at different times. She goes on to say that even if our hearts are in the right place, that does not necessarily allow us to figure out how to navigate the campus to get things accomplished. Carole admitted that she is proudest of what she has done early in her career when there were major obstacles to overcome, such as inserting power door operators and constructing ramps, and, later, when in conversation with architects and civil engineers to see what can be done differently, new buildings were made accessible so that retrofitting was no longer necessary. Relationships with people are a key factor, she stated, and there is never an excuse not to move forward with accessibility features despite the often huge funding expenses involved. Carole has had her emotional moments, as well, especially when it came to accommodations for employees or students. A new ramp for North Quad, an accessible door for Mendelssohn Theater—these were just a few of the noteworthy accomplishments during Carole's tenure as U-M's ADA coordinator. And Carole herself admitted, she does not make the curb cuts nor install power door operators but works closely with the campus civil engineers and plant employees to accomplish these positive accessibility changes to make sure that there is equity and inclusion for everyone. She concluded by thanking the council for its support over the years. Carole's position as ADA Coordinator was soon filled by Christina Kline of that Office. Anthony Walesby, Director of OIE, resigned a little after Carole left U-M, and his post was taken by Pamela Heatlie.

SSD and Other Campus Partners

If statistics are taken into consideration and depending on one's definition of "disability," the number of individuals with disabilities in the United States is said to be one in five or 20% of the population. On our own campus, we have more than 2,000 students who are registered with SSD, but it is suspected that there are many more students, as well as staff and faculty members, who, for one reason or another, do not reveal their disabilities, and, of course, the council and the disability community respect that right.

The Office of the Services for Students with Disabilities (always known as "SSD") was established at the university a decade before the council was formed. Although complementary and collaborative units, they serve quite different functions. SSD has as its mission statement: "To support the University's commitment to equity and diversity by providing support services and academic accommodations to students with disabilities. We share information, promote awareness of disability issues, and provide support of a decentralized system of access for students within the University community." While there are similarities between the council and the SSD in their respective mission statements membership, and while both units are dedicated to students with disabilities, the major difference is that SSD is an official U-M entity established through and abiding by federal and University Standard Practice Handbook regulations, whereas the council is an advocacy service for everyone: all levels of campus employees, visitors, and the local community, as well as hospital patients.

Another collaborative partnership is with the Ann Arbor District Library (AADL) with whom the council committee schedules an event or two annually during the Investing in Ability series. In addition to partnering with the University Health Service's CRP, we have cooperated with the U-M CRLT, another campus organization that presents a workshop on a mutual theme at every October's Investing in Ability series; popular CRLT workshop themes have been centered on classroom inclusivity and accessibility for all students.

Outside the walls of the university, another one of our partners is the Ann Arbor Center for Independent Living, an organization with which the council has many common members as well as mutual goals. We have also worked on collaborative events with the U-M CRP and with Dawn Farm, a Michigan addiction treatment center, a few years ago, to disseminate information about resources related to addiction. The CRP provides support and friendship to U-M students in recovery from addiction, and Dawn Farm places emphasis on the local recovering community as the most important source of healing and recovery.

Welcoming Language and Etiquette—Council's Sample Letter to be Distributed by a U-M Professor to His/Her Students, with Explanatory Preface

The purpose of the letter is multi-fold: To increase appropriate accommodations for students with disabilities. To facilitate communication between students and faculty about disability and accommodation. To help both students and faculty feel more comfortable discussing disability and accommodation by providing as starting point. To encourage students to bring request for accommodation forward earlier rather than later. To remind both faculty and students that it is ordinarily the student's responsibility to initiate requests for accommodation. To enable faculty to feel comfortable including language about accommodation. To remind faculty that it is standard practice to provide accommodation to students with disabilities. To suggest that there are a variety of ways in which courses may be modified to accommodate students with disabilities. To assure faculty that the burden of determine accommodation does not fall on them alone. To remind faculty that the determination of accommodation may not rest solely with them. To identify the Services for Students with Disabilities as a resource to both students and faculty. To remind faculty that information about a student's disability is sensitive and should be treated with discretion; to increase the likelihood that faculty will actually use the language in their syllabi; and to accomplish all this in a short, clear prose:

Accommodation for Students with Disabilities (letter).

If you need or desire an accommodation for a disability, I encourage you to contact me at your earliest convenience. Many aspects of this course, the assignments, the in-class activities, and the way that I teach can be modified to facilitate your participation and program throughout the semester. The earlier you make me aware of your needs, the more effectively we will be able to use the resources available to us, such as the Services for Students with Disabilities, the Adaptive Technology Computing Site, and the life [like]. If you do decide to disclose your disability, I will (to the extent permitted by law) treat that information as private and confidential.

Kudos and Compliments to the Council
from Several Current Council Members

1. I have appreciated and enjoyed my affiliation with the Council for Disability Concerns and the important work that this committee does. Again, thank you for all the inspiring work that is done on behalf of our campus community. I learned much from serving on the committee. (From an Undergraduate Admissions officer upon her retirement in June, 2017)

This is my contribution to the CFDC collection of impressions and history:

I have had the opportunity to be as part of the Council for Disability Concerns for many years. During that time our membership has grown tremendously. We have come to be widely recognized as an essential part of the U of M community. Voices of university students, faculty, and staff as well as Ann Arbor Community members are always welcome and respected.

The CFDC facilitates conversations with collective wisdom that offers creative solutions to challenges, enhancement of resources, and the promotion of successful healthy living for both persons with disabilities and our community. The council hosts a meeting place for dedicated people to exchange ideas and facilitate the changes that have made Ann Arbor a better place to live, study, and work. Our focus has always been on equitable life enhancement through awareness, education, inclusion, positive change, and respect for people with disabilities and their contributions.

The CFDC Abilities Week is now Abilities Month and more. The activities highlight the accomplishments of many and offer opportunities for education about human diversity and community engagement.

All are welcome!

2. I love that the council is a voice for those who are afraid to use their voice.

3. The council makes U-M a much better place to work and learn. Bravo!

4. The council serves as a "Think Tank" for campus disability issues.

5. The council has been a valuable source of information. I have only been attending for about 8 months and it has altered my life in such a positive way.

6. New here, came to talk about ME/CFS, stayed to listen and learn.

7. I am learning about many other kinds of disabilities (By a visually-impaired member)

8. Get rid of that scoundrel Jack Bernard. (By Jack Bernard, the Chair, himself)

9. I have never taken an "upper" nor smoked marijuana in my life, but I imagine the "high" effect would be the way I feel after each council meeting.

10. You all have done such amazing work. I am so proud of the group. (By the retiring director of U-M housing)

Cultural Changes on Campus Effected by the Council about Disability

We believe that most thoughtful people will agree that while advances in technology to improve life for those with disabilities are tremendously impressive and are occurring rapidly, changing the culture is an inordinately difficult, if not impossible, challenge and therefore must be a perennially ongoing, sustained mission. As a result, the council has had to be innovative, planning about how to capture the community's attention and thereby by gentle advocacy sometimes to change minds and hearts. We have tried to do this through partnerships, through sponsoring athletic activities, through referrals and support, through community building, and through providing education and inspiration on campus. We believe that although council members meet for only one hour, once a month throughout the year, the long-term team effort of the U-M CFDC has been effective in making a positive, innovative change in the cultural attitude toward disability issues on campus and thus in definitely enhancing it.

In the over thirty years of its existence, these changes have been gradual but consistently incremental; however, in recent years, the council has truly come into its own and, we believe, has had a ripple effect campus-wide. Through its annual outreach, educational, advocacy, and destigmatizing presented in the annual Investing in Ability series of events, the council is reaching out and influencing other campus units. This effort has been officially recognized in a Regents' Meeting in recent years. Council members are particularly grateful in having had a number of "champions" among the Regents over the years. They have all been reachable and receptive to the progress being made in the area of accessibility on campus. We feel very hopeful that these changes will continue in that we are envisioning a future innovative shift of the entire campus culture in which disability will become an accepted part of diversity, in which universal design will be automatically integrated in every campus plan and building design, and in which there will be total accessibility for everyone and nobody will feel stigmatized or marginalized because of physical, mental, emotional, or cognitive differences. These are, and continue to be, the important "outside the Cube" goals of the U-M CFDC. We also hope, naturally, that what we have done to date and continue to do as a council can be applied to other institutions. While changes in culture can never be readily quantified or evaluated on a financial basis, in our particular area of interest, the rewards come in terms of improved daily living for all those in our campus community and thereby making the University of Michigan an even better place. In addition, we believe that our goals can be replicated elsewhere, and we would very much like to serve as a model for as many other universities as possible. And the council work continues . . .

Appendix A

A Detailed Example of a Typical Investing in Ability Program

Theme: Outreach Series on Stigma, Stereotypes, and Bullying: An Academic Model

ABSTRACT

The University of Michigan Council for Disability Concerns presents Investing in Ability, an annual program of events every October based on a specific theme with the goal of educating via outreach, destigmatizing disability and emphasizing accessibility for everyone, regardless of mental or physical challenges. Previous themes have involved invisible disabilities, accessible architecture, recovery from substance abuse, and honoring veterans. In 2015, in conjunction with a campus-wide initiative, the council members presented a series of events revolving around obstacles to diversity, equity, and inclusion. These events focused on the concepts of stigma, stereotypes, and bullying.

INTRODUCTION

A new initiative on diversity, equity, and inclusion, instituted in 2015 by President Mark Schlissel of the University of Michigan (U-M), presented an opportunity for the university's Council for Disability Concerns to focus on factors that work against diversity: individuals, particularly those with physical or mental challenges, are marginalized by stigma, stereotyping, or bullying (https://record.umich.edu/articles/president-schlissel-kicks-campuswide-effort-improve-diversity).

METHODS

Every October, the month dedicated nationwide to disability, the U-M's Council for Disability Concerns stages a number of events known as "Investing in Ability" that are based on a different theme each year. The goal of this series of presentations is to educate and destigmatize disability issues as well as to promote and raise consciousness about the Council's existence on campus. Whereas last year's theme had been related to substance abuse ("Is Addiction a Disability?") and the previous year, the events were related to invisible disabilities (https://ssd.umich.edu/article/2015-investing-ability-stigma-stereotypes-and; Schnitzer, 2015), 2015 was selected as the year to present an inclusive series of events on "Stigma, Stereotypes, and Bullying." These are behaviors that are painful to many, especially individuals in the disability community. Since they are deemed to be dominant obstacles to the important campus-wide initiative established for the future, it was decided that the concepts of stigma, stereotypes, and bullying needed to be openly and seriously addressed, with examples, in an effort to achieve the university's stated goals of diversity, equity, and inclusion (Zapf & Einarsen, 2010).

Selection of the Theme for Investing in Ability and Formation of the Committee

After the central theme of stigma, stereotypes, and bullying had been established to every member's satisfaction, a committee of about a dozen volunteers from several campus units was formed with its members meeting on a biweekly basis from the beginning of the year, to decide what to include in the calendar of events to most effectively promote the chosen theme. Several of the planned events were quite easily selected immediately, while subsequent ideas and strategies presented themselves in serendipitous ways as the Committee convened to meet throughout the year to discuss further plans.

Reservation of Speakers and Selection of Venues

An important priority that the committee members faced almost immediately was to reserve the venues for the events, because the month of October is always a busy one on campus, and appropriate locations are hard to find unless one acts quickly well in advance. The goal was to hold the events in a variety of places and at convenient times, so that there would be a greater likelihood of attracting a diverse audience. The Committee also needed to decide what dates and times were preferred for the intended presentations. Next, it had to determine whom to invite and then, of course, proceed to invite the selected individuals and groups and find out who was willing to participate and which times and dates would be convenient for each.

The Topics of Stigma and Stereotyping

With stereotyping and stigma as a focus, the first invitation was sent to a physician, a psychiatrist from another university, who was a Muslim and was therefore very conversant with Muslim culture. The university is located in an area very close to a large Muslim community. Her name and interests having been obtained through a simple Internet search for such an expert in the Committee's geographic vicinity, the plan was to invite her to speak on the topic of "Stigma about Mental Illness in the Muslim Community." She agreed to be part of the program.

Next, two linguistics professors were invited to discuss the impact of language on stigma and stereotypes. The first contact was made to one of the professors, a neighbor of a committee member, and this professor invited her department chair to come along to present the lecture as a team effort. Both of these professors were well known to be very popular with their students; in addition, one has both a weekly radio segment and a monthly journal column, so the Committee was reassured that they could also be speaking to a mixed audience on a down-to-earth level rather than a purely academic one.

The important university and college-wide emerging topic of "First Generation" students was included in this series. These "First Gen" students are thought to face stigma because of their special situations. The first in their families to attend college, many of these students had already formed and joined a support group on campus because of the factors they had in common (http://chronicle.com/article/The-Challenge-of-the/230137/). The Committee determined that a panel discussion would be the best format for this particular subject. The thought was that this panel would be able to describe their particular problems and suggest solutions to some of the accessibility obstacles encountered on becoming integrated into academic life. This panel, as part of the diversity movement, would also potentially be helpful to the university administration and future "First Gen" students on campus as well as to the professors and librarians who interacted with them.

A different panel of students was invited to narrate their experiences with mental health issues and concerns. It was noted that there already happened to be an active group of students on campus interested in mental health issues, who were eager to present their personal narratives. These half-a-dozen students held a rehearsal of what each would say to adhere to the one-hour time frame that had been proposed by the program organizers. The panel itself chose the title: "Changing the Conversation about Mental Health." To supplement and balance this student panel, the Committee decided that it would be best to have an additional panel of official university "helping" professionals, psychologists, and social workers to provide a different approach as well as information about available employee and student psychological resources and assistance programs. The expert panel would immediately follow the students' narrative of their personal experiences and would work with the title "Ask Me If I'm Okay: Conversations about Mental Illness in the Workplace."

Since mental health was deemed to be an integral area of stigmatization, a local hospital social worker who specializes in suicide prevention was included in the list of invitees for another presentation. She would describe her experiences with affected patients and give a summary of reasons for and prevention of suicidal ideation. This talk seemed to the Committee to be important for future social workers and therefore was scheduled to be held in the School of Social Work Conference Room. A box lunch provided by the School was available for all audience members as an extra incentive to attend.

The Committee also invited a well-known lawyer who is a visually impaired disability advocate. He had spoken previously to an audience from the disability community and therefore could be counted on to provide spirit and inspiration to the audience interested in issues concerning stigma in a very positive way. In addition to narrating his struggles to obtain his law degree and telling about his experiences and the work he is currently involved with, he would describe his impressive athletic achievements and also his recovery from a recent serious accident. For this event, the committee planned to provide a pizza lunch for everyone.

The members of the Investing in Ability Committee added several other events as the planning progressed and as further ideas for the schedule coalesced. One of these, inserted at almost the last minute, focused on stigma in comics and graphic novels interwoven with medical information. This presentation built on an exhibit that was concurrently taking place at a public library in a nearby town. The panel consisted of university librarians and representatives from two local public libraries, all of whom were comics and graphic novel aficionados. Those panelists would point out that the alter ego of a number of the superheroes had disabilities and were stigmatized as a result with a subsequent dramatic resolution as they changed personas. There would also be an exhibit of relevant material to correspond to the presentation.

Another occasion to present a scenario of diversity that countered stigma and stereotypes involved the showing of a documentary called *Including Samuel*, a film directed and created by a university alumnus. The Committee had requested in advance that the Library purchase this item for its institutional collection. The film was shown in a convenient Library venue at the lunch hour break (https://www.includingsamuel .com).

The hosts of a visiting author requested that she be included in the Investing in Ability events, which the Committee was happy to agree to. She had been invited and sponsored by several different departments for her talk on "Where the Light Gets In: Writing from the Margin," describing how her deafness inspired and assisted her in telling her story (https://events.umich.edu/event/24087).

Another program that was scheduled late in the month was a reading of their own poetry by two members of the disability community. These poet performers would share their experiences of disability through embodied texts engaging the stigma of mental health differences and the poetic histories of representing pain. For several past years, the Committee has also presented an art exhibit, because a persistent goal was to include some type of artistic expression for every Investing in Ability series. Because an appropriate, accessible venue could not be located for an art exhibit this time, the Committee agreed that poetic reading on the topic of disability from a personal viewpoint would be the art of choice for 2015. Gradually, the interstices of the month's schedule began to close up until there were few, if any, dates left to be filled in.

The Topic of Bullying in a Hospital Workplace

The Committee wanted to incorporate a lecture on bullying in the workplace and to hold this presentation in an auditorium of the University of Michigan Hospital (now Michigan Medicine) that, although separate physically, is an integral part of the university structure. Large medical institutions, generally speaking, are known to be hierarchical in nature; therefore, the objective of this talk was to address the type of culture that might be conducive to bullying among various levels of the medical profession. About eight years previously, an expert from an outside university had been invited to speak on this topic of bullying in the workplace, also at this same university hospital. At that time, her tips in her talk about resisting bullying had been very favorably received by an audience that consisted primarily of nurses; therefore, the committee decided to ask her to return to present her PowerPoint lecture to the medical staff once again.

Because in addition to being found in the workplace, bullying often occurs in schools, upon the strong recommendation of a teacher acquainted with one of the council members, the Committee invited a local high school's basketball coach who was known for setting up a successful "no bullying" policy. This particular presentation would be held in the local public library to encourage the public to attend and would be a collaborative effort with the library. The coach agreed to include a panel of students and a school counselor at this event. Publicity for this event would be posted on the library's excellent website.

Modeling Diversity in the Classroom

Every year, the CRLT, another university unit, collaborates with the Committee by presenting a workshop on the theme selected for that year. This interactive mini-workshop is primarily intended for Graduate Student Assistants but is also open to others; it requires registration in advance because it fills up quickly, usually with a lengthy waiting list. The curriculum is a microcosm of a semester's worth of instruction on inclusive teaching and fair treatment to all individuals, regardless of their physical and/or mental differences. The workshop this year, grounded in Universal Design by Learning (UDL), explored the ways in which technology can support learning but also some of the barriers created. The instructors worked through a couple of case studies on using technology in the classroom and provided participants with an opportunity to revise or create an assignment to make it more accessible (http://www.crlt.umich.edu/gsis/p3_1).

Dogs . . . Dogs . . . Dogs

For the past decade, the Committee, initially with contacts through Paws with a Cause, has extended an annual invitation to various organizations of therapy dogs, service dogs, and pups-in-training; the animals assemble with their owners and fostering parents on the central area of the campus. It is always an uplifting, well-attended festive parade of many assorted dogs and their accompanying human beings. Most students passing through this area, known as "The Diag," between classes are immediately attracted to the animals, and this convergence serves as an ideal occasion for Committee members to pass out flyers for the various events that they plan to hold during the following days. Over the years, in addition to the service dogs, owners of therapy dogs and other types of assistance dogs have joined the group. Consequently, a number of other campus venues have been added for dog viewing: the main hospital, an outlying medical campus, and an administrative building. This particular ongoing event is intended to celebrate the ways that a person with a disability gains independence along with a substantially increased quality of life with a service dog. In conjunction with this, for several past years, a lecturer from the School of Social Work has given a talk on the animal-human bond. In addition, this occasion raises awareness about the value of dogs, causing a ripple effect on campus; now therapy dogs are being invited to various libraries to decrease student stress during exams (https://www.pawswithacause.org/).

At the very end of the series of Investing in Ability events, as sort of a grand finale, there is a very festive Army-Navy Wheelchair Basketball Game established to honor all the veterans in the community, including student-veterans, and also the members of the disability community. For this free event, the Committee invites the entire community, including all students, local scout, and charitable organizations, as well as patients at the local Veterans Administration Hospital. The Game participants include both wheelchair users, several of whom are paralympians, along with students and veterans who do not regularly use wheelchairs. One of the Committee members has been the chief planner, organizer, and presenter of this game for the past ten years, and it has grown bigger and more celebratory each year to the point that now the sideline coaching and entertainment crew includes the University Dance Team, University Cheerleaders, and several of the University basketball team members along with their coach. A disc jockey plays live music, and an Army band is also part of the colorful spectacle. There is always a military display by the Color Guard from the University's Reserved Officers Training Corps (ROTC) and an Honorary Marshall. Past Honorary Marshalls have included a Congressman, a University Regent, and a number of well-known athletic team coaches (https://deanofstudents.umich.edu/article/um-army-vs-navy-wheelchair-basketball-game).

At the conclusion of the October events, there is an annual recognition ceremony, the James T. Neubacher Award, established to acknowledge those university members nominated by others for special achievements in the area of disability. Nominees can be either individuals or groups but have to be affiliates: faculty, staff, students, or alumni of the university. One individual or group from the list of nominees is chosen to be awarded a special plaque and an honorarium from the President's Office. A University Regent presents the plaque and introduces the main awardee, who also gives a short speech. Up to twenty-five Certificates of Appreciation are presented to the other nominees with a brief description of why each is being recognized. A Continental breakfast is available for all attendees and a light luncheon is offered to the guests by invitation. A certain amount of planning is involved for this event, and a separate, smaller unit of members coordinates it (http://ability.umich.edu/iaw/neubacher.html).

Financing

As far as financial support is concerned, recently the committee has succeeded in obtaining a small revolving fund to pay for room reservations, plus a minimal amount of food, some token gifts to speakers, printing of programs, and miscellaneous expenses. The committee receives some support from the University Health System as well. For the Army-Navy Wheelchair Basketball Game, which is held in a major sports complex and for which the rent and other expenses are high, the Committee has received funding from two private sources but, inevitably because of the expense of this ever-growing project, must always seek further support.

Reaching Out to a Distant Campus

An additional goal for the Committee this year was to coordinate with and broadcast some of the events to a distant campus unit via a conferencing mechanism, an activity that required expertise from outside the Committee. This year, two of the presentations were scheduled to be video-cast, a second attempt since the previous year the reception for this distance activity had not worked well. The stakeholders on the other campus were becoming discouraged, but with practice and an improved technical setup, the Committee hoped that the transmission this time would be more successful.

Publicity

As soon as the schedule appeared to be complete, the Committee members met with the Human Resources Communications Department representative who was willing to provide a template with an appropriate design for the flyers intended for use for publicity. This individual also worked with the Committee to create a website with details of the numerous events. The Committee members themselves were responsible for distributing the finished flyers via a template and for contacting local media to request that events be publicized. The members also used the social media of Facebook and Twitter and traditional email to send information to groups and individuals who might be interested in attending the events. Large-screen advertisements provided by Human Resources and a hospital publicist were dispersed around the campus.

RESULTS

The Committee created an evaluation form for the events, a short and simple one that was nonacademic in style, to find out specifically how the audience members learned about the event and whether they enjoyed and/or learned from it. From this feedback, the Committee learned that most participants had been alerted by an email message, although some had also read about a happening on a website or had been informed by a friend or colleague through word of mouth. The feedback reinforced the selection of this year's theme of stigma, stereotyping, and bullying. The preponderance of the responses were extremely positive, with the lectures on linguistics and bullying in the workplace being particular audience favorites. Participants requested that the PowerPoint slides of several of the lectures be sent to them, especially the ones on bullying in the workplace and the impact of language. It was suggested in their evaluations by several participants that some topics could be expanded into a series of presentations or an ongoing workshop. Apart from the attendance at the Army-Navy Wheelchair Game, which consisted of over 1,000, the largest audiences were the ones for the linguistics lecture, for which seventy people were present on site and thirty at the teleconferenced location, and for the James T. Neubacher Award Ceremony, where a hundred people showed up. The average number of audience members ranged between forty and sixty at each event. The total number of participants in the series was approximately 500, with an estimated 1,000 at the Army-Navy Wheelchair Game.

One of the audience members was able to provide a "storification" of a number of the events. This process consisted of tweeting the main concepts of each lecture or panel discussion and adding value by including relevant background information. One of the benefits of this method was that asynchronous, long-term access would be available to individuals and communities unable to attend the events in person (see Examples of Storification after Readings).

DISCUSSION

The theme of the 2015 Investing in Ability series of events was intended to reinforce the university's all-campus initiative by exposing stigma, stereotypes, and bullying as causes that impede the goals of diversity, equity, and inclusion. As a result of the month's events, the Committee achieved more than 1,000 individual interactions with emphasis on the aforementioned factors. Although outcomes in this project are intangible and could be determined primarily by the audience members' evaluations submitted at each event, the feedback, to a satisfying extent, was both enthusiastic and positive, strengthening the Committee's belief that Investing in Ability, although it takes quite a bit of time and preplanning, is well worth the effort. Acknowledging that building the case for the need and success of this program requires strong stakeholder support, the Investing in Ability Committee is planning to continue its mission of stressing diversity, equity, and inclusion on campus in 2016.

Lessons Learned

- Committee planning for events must take place well in advance, especially with respect to reserving locations and inviting busy guest speakers.
- Collaborative efforts and alliances with other interested units are paramount in carrying out the program, attracting audiences, achieving desired results from events, and delivering the essential messages.
- Publicity is a vital element for the series of events, and every opportunity should be taken advantage of to spread the word via flyers, daily email reminders, posting on campus venues, radio broadcasts, social media, and general word-of-mouth networking to both individuals and organizations.
- Storification can be a valuable asset for interested individuals who cannot be present in person when the events cannot be video-taped. If a volunteer in the audience agrees to tweet the program,

those results are very helpful in enriching the content and in the dissemination of information from each talk.

- Expert technical assistance is critical for conferencing set-ups, and those persons instrumental in setting up the systems probably need to have at least one rehearsal beforehand to avoid technical glitches.

READINGS

Carter, B. B., & Spencer, V. G. (2006). The fear factor: Bullying and students with disabilities. *International Journal of Special Education, 21,* 11–23.

Greenstein, L. (2015). 9 ways to fight mental health stigma. *National Alliance for the Mentally Ill-NAMI Blog.* Retrieved from https://www.nami.org/Blogs/NAMI-Blog/October-2015/9-Ways-to-Fight-Mental-Health-Stigma#

Halverson, D. (2010). *Workplace abuse in the medical workplace: Fact vs myth.* Workplace Bullying Institute. Retrieved from http://www.workplacebullying.org/tag/halverson/

Iseler, J. (2015, February 16). *President Schlissel kicks off campuswide effort to improve diversity.* The University Record: News for Faculty and Staff. Retrieved from Nansel, T. R., Overpeck, M., Pilla, R. S., Ruan, W. J., Simons-Morton, B., & Scheidt, P. (2001). Bullying behaviors among US youth: Prevalence and association with psychosocial adjustment. *Journal of the American Medical Association, 285,* 2094–2100. Retrieved from http://www.ncbi.nlm.nih.gov/pmc/articles/PMC2435211/

Pinel, E. C., Warner, L. R., & Chua, P. P. (2005). Getting there is only half the battle: Stigma consciousness and maintaining diversity in higher education. *Journal of Social Issues, 61,* 481–506. http://dx.doi.org/10.1111/j.1540-4560.2005.00417.x

Roberson, Q. M. (2004). *Disentangling the meanings of diversity and inclusion in organizations* (CAHRS Working Paper 04-05). Ithaca, NY: Cornell University, School of Industrial and Labor Relations, Center for Advanced Human Resource Studies. Retrieved from http://digitalcommons.ilr.cornell.edu/cahrswp/12

Schnitzer, A. E. (2015). Outreach to addiction—A month of investing in ability: A case study. *Medical Reference Services Quarterly, 34,* 334–342. http://dx.doi.org/10.1080/02763869.2015.1052694

Zapf, D. (1999). Organisational, work group related and personal causes of mobbing/bullying at work. *International Journal of Manpower, 20,* 70–85. http://dx.doi.org/10.1108/01437729910268669

Examples of Storifications Captured by Patricia F. Anderson

Bullying in the Workplace: http://hdl.handle.net/2027.42/142402.

Impact of Language on Stigma and Stereotypes: http://hdl.handle.net/2027.42/142402.

James T. Neubacher Award Ceremony: http://hdl.handle.net/2027.42/ 142402.

Muslim Stigma/Mental Health: http://hdl.handle.net/2027.42/142402.

REFERENCES

Schnitzer, A. E. (2015). Outreach to addiction—A month of investing in ability: A case study. *Medical Reference Services Quarterly, 54*, 334–342.

Zapf, D., & Einarsen, S. (2010, September 10). Bullying in the workplace: Recent trends in research and practice—An introduction. *European Journal of Work and Organizational Policy.* Retrieved from http://www.tandfonline.com/doi/ abs/10.1080/13594320143000807

Appendix B

Detailed Minutes of a Meeting

Minutes: Council for Disability Concerns, July 11, 2017—typical one-hour meeting

ATTENDING

Jack Bernard, Chair; Anna Ercoli Schnitzer, Coordinator; Patricia Anderson, Scribe; Susan Barnes; Janet Keller; Cathy Alice Koyanagi; Lloyd Shelton; Kathleen Mozak-Betts; Jim Eng; Martin Warin; Jim Cherney; Randi Johnson; Stephanie Rosen; Bonnie Dede; Todd Austin; Jason Apap; Chris Taylor. Logging in remotely via BlueJeans: Brad Eberhoeh and Suzanne Bade; Dianna Woods; Alex Kazarooni; Taimi Megivern; Renee Saulter; Tracy Wright; Emily Dibble

ANNOUNCEMENTS

Cathy Alice:

Toastmasters (nonprofit)

Location for training on August 18—looking for venue

Fifty people—big main room

Three break out rooms (20 ea)

Anna:

Excellent session on disability and ADA by Christina; she and Stephanie will collaborate on Library session; Christina willing to present other sessions or speak to individuals personally regarding disability/accessibility/accommodations.

Description of Joelle Fundaro's Career Clothes Closet for undergraduates (seeking "gently used clothing for interviewing")

Handouts:

- Center for Independent Living (three handouts)
- Ten Tips for Inclusive Meetings
- Clothing Drive for the Career Center
- Flyer for Investing in Ability events

Martin:

Lobby for a film documentary for Investing in Ability

UnRest

http://www.unrest.film/

Trailer: https://www.youtube.com/watch?v=MWIc9mKedF4 (see Photo 15)

TED Talk: https://www.youtube.com/watch?v=Fb3yp4uJhq0

Topic: Myalgic Encephalomyelitis/Chronic Fatigue Syndrome (ME/CFS): https://prevention.nih.gov/programs-events/pathways-to-prevention/workshops/me-cfs

Potential Campus Partners:

- CFDC
- Investing in Ability
- UMInDS
- ScreenArts
- School of Art and Design?
- Women's studies
- Already have MICHR and $70 pledged toward $250 showing of film, Unrest

Possible Discussion Panel:

- Possible Discussion panel with Petra Kuppers and a filmmaker
- https://www.chronicle.com/article/The-Neglected-Demographic-/240439

Photo 15 Preview YouTube video UnRest (documentary about ME/CFS) premiere on Sundance Film Festival—January 19, 2017

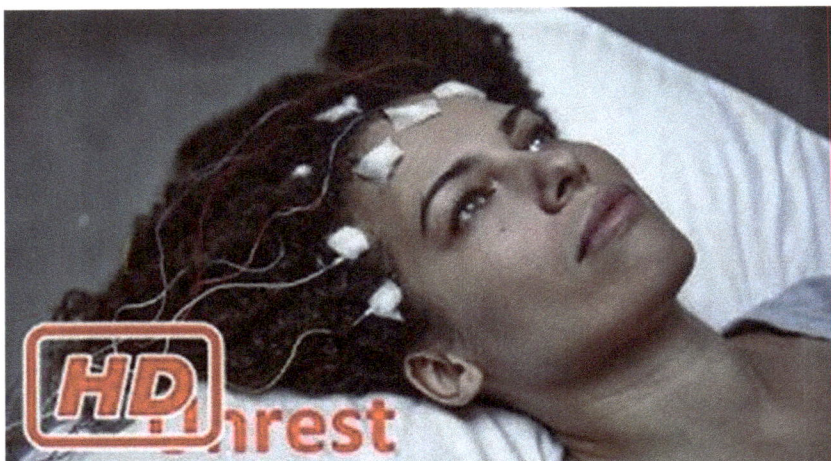

AGENDA

Stephanie Rosen

Coordinating accommodations for faculty and staff at U-M

The Neglected Demographic: Faculty Members with Disabilities

By Joseph Grigely, June 27, 2017

https://www.chronicle.com/article/The-Neglected-Demographic-/240439

Most colleges have offices for students with disabilities, but no similar resource for faculty or staff. Are they able to progress through the tenure and promotion process in an equitable fashion?

Story: How This Has Come up in the Library

- Providing access through HathiTrust (Jack described)
- Collection of digitized works from academic libraries
- 14 million volumes now
- They were previously inaccessible, but now made available in accessible formats
- Ways in which higher education is now making these available to persons with print disabilities
- Everyone at U-M has access to most, students with print disabilities have access to ALL
- Now, the new challenge was a faculty member with a print disability who wanted access.
- There was no office to manage the verification service.
- This highlighted a gap in service for the faculty.
- The library wants to provide appropriate levels of service for EVERYONE on campus.
- The discovery that faculty and staff may be excluded from certain parts of service because of these gaps in coverage and support for disabilities has been a revelation.
- Council advocated for centralized resources for students, but there is no centralized resource for faculty or staff.

Who Should Be Involved in Creating this Type of Service?

- Office for Institutional Equity (Christina **Kline**)
- Campus HR
- Academic HR
- MHealthy (Sue Bade)
- Services for Students with Disabilities (Stuart **Segal** et al.)

- Michigan Medicine Disability (Clarissa Love/Michelle Meade)— Subcommittee already working on accommodations for employees/ hospital patients
- Work Connections

Discussion ensued, more robustly that I could capture.

Relevant Resources:

Change in Ability to Work (Sue Bade)—Council site has link to this information

https://hr.umich.edu/benefits-wellness/health-well-being/mhealthy/ occupational-health/change-ability-work

PDF: https://hr.umich.edu/sites/default/files/change-in-ability-to-work .pdf

Resources: https://hr.umich.edu/benefits-wellness/health/mhealthy/occu pational-health/change-ability-work/change-ability-work-resources

Americans with Disabilities Act Information: https://hr.umich.edu/ working-u-m/workplace-improvement/office-institutional-equity/ americans-disabilities-act-information

Physical Change in Ability to Work: https://hr.umich.edu/benefits- wellness/health/mhealthy/occupational-health/change-ability-work/ physical-change-ability-work

Jack Bernard on Service Animals

Increase in requests to accommodate service animals on campus. Dramatic, record setting increase. Not so many problems with "service animals" that have been trained for a specific or general purpose, but ESA (Emotional Support Animals) that need no special certification nor training but are allowed in the dorms by Fair Housing Act. Service animals can be only dogs or miniature horses but ESA can be almost any animal from snakes to mongooses.

Policies began with service animals for vision impairment, shifted to mobility, the deafness, and now more complex and subtle. New options include epilepsy, diabetes, mental health, dietary needs, comfort animals (PTSD, anxiety disorders, etc.). Department of Justice has given confusing guidance on these issues. Disabled Student Services in Higher Education (DSSHE), a national listserv on various disability topics, has an ongoing discussion regarding ESA.

Inclusion of service animals is complicated.

Cathy Alice Gave Examples

Guide dogs used as guard dogs

Guide dogs used to get attention

Guide dogs used appropriately as guide dogs

People pushing the limits

Need for real limits

For diabetes, continuous glucose monitors can be alternatives to alert dogs (this can be debated)

http://www.diabeticalertdogsofamerica.com/service

http://www.healthline.com/health/type-2-diabetes/dogs

ESA—Emotional Support Animals

Bearded dragon: http://www.wacotrib.com/waco_today_magazine/teenager-s-bearded-dragon-helps-ease-her-anxiety/article_644f1a32-ea54-5c59-8415-783882eec780.html

Hamster: https://www.biggerpockets.com/forums/52/topics/285126-really---is-there-such-a-thing-as-a-service-hamster

Challenges balancing animal phobias and allergies with accommodations for ESAs. Can't segregate, must integrate.

Eastern Michigan University (EMU) writing a contract for students with ESA to promise to take responsibility for their animal. Maintenance and well-being of the animal. Validation process is difficult. Who says, "not disabled to this degree." Have to rely on the medical professionals providing the supporting paperwork. Defining boundaries.

Are only service animals allowed who have been trained for a specific function for a person with a disability?

Emotional support animals have no training, no certification. Lots of requests by students to have an ESA.

Analogy

It infuriates us when we see someone take a wheelchair parking spot because they are driving their mother's cars.

"I could qualify for a hanging parking sticker for my car because of my disability. I would never do that because I walk fine. I would never take that resource from someone else who really needs it."

As people with disabilities, we are all stewards of the system.

People tend to function better when we have animals around us. People evolved with animals. This makes it difficult.

"That's okay. I'll just not use my service animal there." [Gasp]

"I'll use my crutches instead of my wheelchair."

Housekeeping Notes Regarding Council Announcements, BlueJeans Remote Conferencing, and Related Upcoming Information

Todd, Jason, and Chris will obtain a permanent phone-in number for our remote users

Jim Eng and Patricia working on a calendar for council, seeking an email address to use

Our thanks to our experts: Todd, Jason and Chris

Our thanks to Patricia for the detailed minutes

These conversations to be continued in the future

Appendix C

Photo 16 Flyer for 2017 Investing in Ability Program

Photo 17 Flyer for U-M CFDC

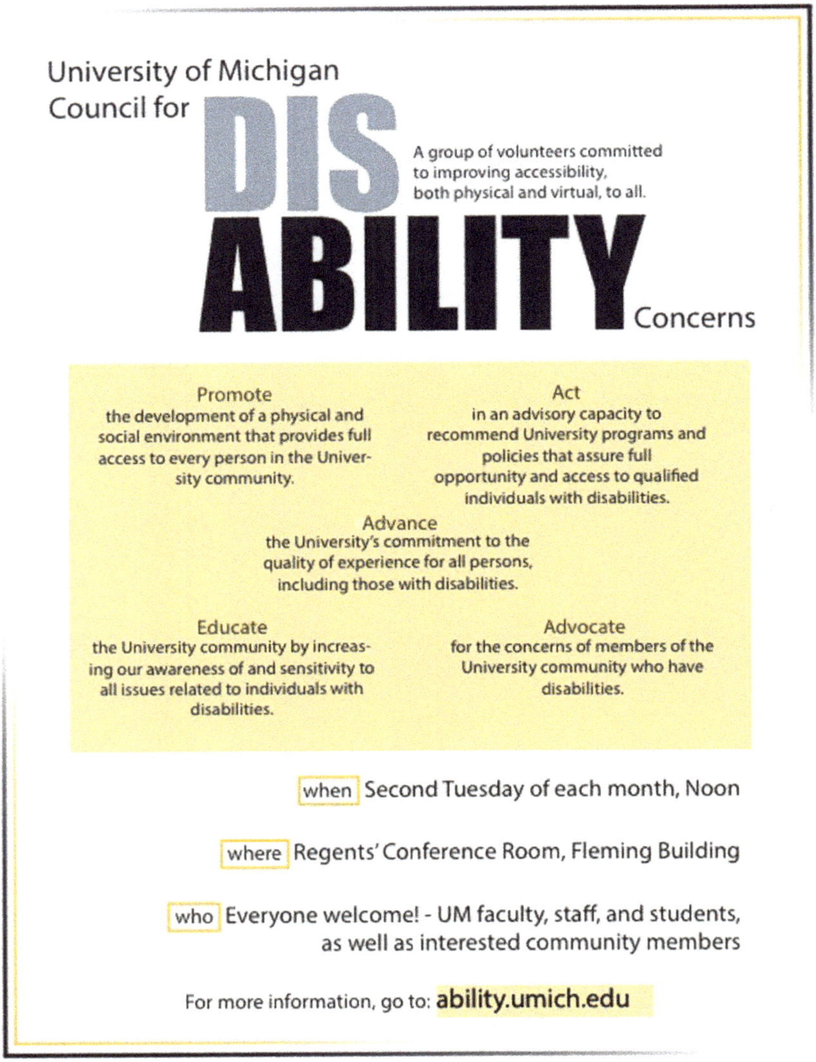

University of Michigan
Council for

DIS

A group of volunteers committed
to improving accessibility,
both physical and virtual, to all.

ABILITY Concerns

Promote
the development of a physical and
social environment that provides full
access to every person in the University community.

Act
in an advisory capacity to
recommend University programs and
policies that assure full
opportunity and access to qualified
individuals with disabilities.

Advance
the University's commitment to the
quality of experience for all persons,
including those with disabilities.

Educate
the University community by increasing our awareness of and sensitivity to
all issues related to individuals with
disabilities.

Advocate
for the concerns of members of the
University community who have
disabilities.

when Second Tuesday of each month, Noon

where Regents' Conference Room, Fleming Building

who Everyone welcome! - UM faculty, staff, and students,
as well as interested community members

For more information, go to: **ability.umich.edu**

Index

www.ingramcontent.com/pod-product-compliance
Lightning Source LLC
Chambersburg PA
CBHW051430270326
41933CB00022B/3483